# Classical Japanese Cinema Revisited

D1438345

# Classical Japanese Cinema Revisited

*Catherine Russell*

continuum

The Continuum International Publishing Group
80 Maiden Lane, New York, NY 10038
The Tower Building, 11 York Road, London SE1 7NX

www.continuumbooks.com

Copyright © 2011 by Catherine Russell

Library of Congress Cataloging-in-Publication Data
Russell, Catherine, 1959-
Classical Japanese cinema revisited / by Catherine Russell.
    p. cm.
  Includes bibliographical references.
  ISBN-13: 978-1-4411-1681-9 (hardcover : alk. paper)
  ISBN-10: 1-4411-1681-8 (hardcover : alk. paper)
  ISBN-13: 978-1-4411-3327-4 (pbk. : alk. paper)
  ISBN-10: 1-4411-3327-5 (pbk. : alk. paper) 1. Motion pictures—Japan—History—
20th century. I. Title.
  PN1993.5.J3R87 2011
  791.430952'0904—dc22                    2010043687

ISBN:  978-1-4411-1681-9 (hardback)
       978-1-4411-3327-4 (paperback)

Typeset by Pindar NZ, Auckland, New Zealand
Printed and bound in the United States of America

For Bonnie and Elliot

# Contents

# Acknowledgments

When Richard Porton and Gary Crowdus asked me to review new DVDs of Japanese films for the magazine *Cineaste*, it provided a great opportunity for me to write about some of the classics of Japanese film. I am greatly indebted to the editorial staff at *Cineaste* for their support of this writing. Secondly, the book definitely would not have been possible without the amazing series of Japanese films on DVD that have been released by the Criterion Collection over the years. I would also like to thank Duke University Press for permission to reprint parts of my book about Mikio Naruse. The article that has become the first chapter to the book was originally presented at a workshop on transnational Asian cinemas organized by Tonglin Lu and Meaghan Morris, and is published in *The China Review* and reprinted here with kind permission. The Social Sciences and Humanities Research Council of Canada provided funding for the original research of the Naruse book. Thanks also to Alain Chouinard for assistance in preparing the manuscript for publication.

Catherine Russell
*April, 2011*

The book includes slightly revised selections from the following publications by Catherine Russell:

*The Cinema of Naruse Mikio: Women and Japanese Modernity*. Durham, NC: Duke University Press, 2008.

ix

Review of *The Human Condition*, Criterion Collection DVD, *Cineaste* 35, no. 3 (Summer 2010): 53–5.

Review of *An Autumn Afternoon*, Criterion Collection DVD, *Cineaste* 34, no. 2 (Spring 2009): 83–4.

Review of *Silent Ozu*, Criterion Collection DVDs, *Cineaste* (Fall 2008) web exclusive, available at: http://www.cineaste.com/articles/silent-ozu.htm.

Review of *The Burmese Harp* and *Fires on the Plain*, Criterion Collection DVDs by Kon Ichikawa, *Cineaste* 32, no. 4 (Fall 2007): 63–4.

Review of *Late Spring* DVD, *Cineaste* 32, no. 2 (Spring 2007): 65–7.

Review of *Ugetsu* DVD, *Cineaste* 31, no. 3 (Summer 2006): 64–6.

Review of *A Story of Floating Weeds* and *Floating Weeds* DVD, *Cineaste* 30, no. 1 (Winter 2004): 56–8.

Review of *Tokyo Story* DVD, *Cineaste* 29, no. 3 (Summer 2004): 50–1.

"Men with Swords and Men with Suits: The Cinema of Akira Kurosawa," *Cineaste* 27, no. 1 (Winter 2002): 4–13.

"Japanese Cinema as Classical Cinema," *The China Review*. Special issue edited by Tonglin Lu and Meaghan Morris 10 no. 2, 2010.

# Preface

Who ever said that films were a one-time thing?

Nagisa Oshima

Japanese films have been included among the classics of world cinema ever since 1951 when *Rashomon* (1950) was awarded the Golden Lion at the Venice Film Festival. Embraced by the *Cahiers du Cinéma* critics, numerous titles became canonized as great works of world cinema, exhibiting innovative displays of film technique, a richly poetic vocabulary and universal themes of progressive humanism. In the 1970s, many of these same titles were endorsed as radical alternatives to the dominant norms of classical Hollywood cinema. Japanese cinema of the studio era became a key site of critical discourse, not simply because of its aesthetic values but because its formal language differed significantly from American and European film practices. Moreover, the strong national flavor of this cinema, its auteurist structure and its links to a rich cultural tradition have invited many volumes of critical interpretation.

The classics of Japanese cinema are indubitably beautiful, elegant and extraordinarily well crafted. They have had a significant influence on many international auteurs and genres, especially the action film. And yet, the Japanese cinema that was embraced internationally as a radical alternative to the mainstream was in fact "mainstream" mass entertainment in Japan. From the 1930s through to the early 1960s — the years covered by this book — the Japanese film industry was one of the biggest in the world. It had a well-developed star system and had many highly ranked directors, around whom the system was more or less organized. As more bilingual scholarship reveals and analyzes the complexity of the cultural context of this commercial industry, the "classics" of Japanese cinema can begin to be understood as part of a classical cinema, with all the social, political, historical and ideological implications of the American film industry.

In the American context, "classical" cinema is a critical concept that continues to be in a state of flux. For Bordwell, Staiger and Thompson, it refers to the industrial mode of production that dominated from 1917 to 1960, based on a set of stylistic "rules," or norms, and a set of commercial practices. Even in this sense, the term "classical" is somewhat at odds with the cinema as a form of mass entertainment. "The genius of the system," as André Bazin put it, created the basis from which the auteur cinema came into being. The classicism of cinema includes both the everyday, routine productions that keep the wheels turning and the exceptional masterpieces that can be recognized as artworks. Japanese cinema arguably replicates this classicism in its own terms, with its own methods and "rules" that are not actually that different from those of Hollywood. However, its "group style" emerged from a very different set of cultural and linguistic principles that cannot be reduced to a set of formal rules.

American classical cinema is not merely a style, an art form or a mode of entertainment. It is deeply embedded in the construction of American national subjects — and has come to represent America to other nations (and to Americans themselves). The same can be said of classical Japanese cinema. Film studies scholars have long debated the rhetoric of the classical system as an ideological phenomenon that tends, on one hand, to reproduce assumptions about race, class and gender and, on the other, to constantly question, revise and challenge those conventions, in implicit and explicit ways. Until recently, it has been difficult for non-Japanese audiences to grasp this level of Japanese film, and it is only with the growing numbers of bilingual film scholars able to do original research into Japanese-language sources that the larger picture has begun to come into focus. It has been too easy to imagine the cinema as being representative of a homogeneous national imaginary without fully appreciating the dynamics of power, history and difference that underscore classical Japanese cinema. It wasn't until the 1990s that film scholarship took up a more historical inquiry into the cultural context of these classics. Instead of relating them to archaic cultural forms of "traditional" Japanese culture, critics began to situate them within modern Japanese culture.

As the "classical" cinemas of America and Japan recede in history, they tend to become more circumscribed as coherent styles. They belong to a specific 30-year period of the twentieth century, during which the world underwent huge social, technological and geopolitical changes. My own view of the classical, which will be developed in this book, is not stylistic, but understands it, rather, as a discourse of modernity. As I explain in the first chapter, the American cinema has also begun to be considered in these terms; but I am interested in Japanese modernity as a cultural formation of heterogeneous styles, subjects, discourses and desires. The very question of what is "Japanese" is negotiated in modernity; what one can expect from modernity and how it is experienced are implicit in every film.

The contradictory appellation a "modern classicism" is precisely what interests me about it. The impetus toward a classical style in Japan was an inherently contradictory movement, as cinema was from the outset a discourse of modernity, with all the challenges to established social forms that modernity entailed. However, classical Japanese cinema was intimately involved in negotiating these tensions and constructing a coherent national culture for both domestic and foreign audiences. To the extent that it was based in traditional forms, it was also "inventing tradition" by translating it and framing it in modern terms for modern (heterogeneous and mass) audiences. It thus provides a unique insight into the ideological tensions and emotional challenges of mid-twentieth-century Japanese history.

This book is not a history of Japanese cinema, and is far from being representative or comprehensive of the hundreds of films produced during the studio era. The reader is well advised to consult the many outstanding books that have been written on Japanese cinema from a wide variety of methodological approaches. Japanese film studies is a rich area of film scholarship, partly because it has been developed around engaging debates about Orientalism, modernism, humanism, nationalism and formalism; partly because the films are so rich and partly because the slow process of translation has entailed a constant process of revelation for both Japanese and international scholars. As a national cinema, it poses many critical challenges due to the paucity of materials available from the prewar period — much of which were destroyed during the war — and partly because there is not a great deal of institutional support for the preservation of film culture, or its study, in Japan.

The bulk of this book is made up of reviews of DVDs that were originally published in *Cineaste* magazine between 2001 and 2010. The release of so many key titles in English has enabled an international community to engage with classical Japanese cinema more intensely than ever before. The classical period as I am describing it here is more or less periodized as 1930 to 1960, although studio-produced genre films continued to be made well into the 1960s. As I will explain in the first chapter, the origins of the classical mode are equally imprecise. In any case, the book does tend to overemphasize the 1950s, for a number of reasons, the first of which is that this is the period best represented by the English-language DVD releases. It is sometimes referred to as one of two "golden ages" of Japanese cinema, the other one being the 1930s. During the years following the Occupation, many directors found the first solid footing they'd had since the mid-1930s, when hostilities with China first broke out. It was also a time when generational rifts and cultural clashes were exceedingly tense, as the nation struggled to become a democratic, global player, while simultaneously sublimating war memories and recovering from the huge losses that the war entailed.

Many of the DVD releases — especially the Criterion disks — are supplemented with special features that provide important insights into the production circumstances of the films and the working methods of the directors. These supplements shed new light on the mechanics and ethnography of the Japanese film industry, an area that film scholars have been slow to research and analyze. The chapter on Kurosawa was also originally a review of Stuart Galbraith IV's book *The Emperor and the Wolf* (2001), one of the few books in English to delve into the production history of classical Japanese cinema. The repackaging and rerelease of Japanese cinema in the home theater market has effectively created a new audience with a new kind of access to a cinema that was once rarely screened — and when it was, it was often screened in degraded 16 mm prints. It is in this sense a new and reinvented cinema.

In addition to the DVD reviews, I have included excerpts from my 2008 book on Mikio Naruse. I became interested in this director over 15 years ago, and as I explored the full scope of his 89-film career I began to get a very different picture of the industry as a whole. Naruse may be less stylistically innovative than some of his contemporaries, but his portraits of women were far more respectful of women's agency, subjectivity and values. His films not only depict women's trials and tribulations, which is a very popular topic in Japanese cinema, but also often imply that women should expect more from modernity. This led me to be far more critical of directors such as Ozu and Mizoguchi, whose artistry should not blind us to the way that patriarchal values of Japanese culture tend to be reproduced in their films.

And yet, this book is not intended to be a feminist critique of Japanese cinema, even if some readers may read it that way. It is interpretive and critical, but only in the interests of shedding light on the way that these "classics" engage with social and cultural contradictions, tensions and inequalities. I have tried to be attentive to stylistic traits of these films, with the caveat that, in my view, "style" is not simply a matter of technology — camera movements, editing and lighting — but also a matter of cultural forms. Thus my analyses often make note of architecture, costume and urban space. The cinema is well equipped to make these cultural styles "meaningful" and poetic. In the negotiation and construction of Japanese modernity, the aesthetics of everyday life are highly significant as indices of nationhood, class, gender and generation.

Classical Japanese cinema is a stylish cinema. Each director discussed in this book has their own approach, but there is a consistency of elegant composition, figure placement, use of architecture and lighting design. Elegance in conjunction with the simplicity of everyday life is one of the distinguishing features of this cinema. The stories that unfold are often tales of sorrow, but there is also humor, irony and comedy, in keeping with the goals of a commercial industry to entertain. They are tales of modern life with its many challenges of social transformation, war and new technologies; and they are ways of reimagining the past in keeping with twentieth-century humanist views. The stylishness of the visual field indicates a cultural impetus to aestheticize, to raise the status of everyday life to something more meaningful, more harmonious and more beautiful than, in truth, it really was or could be. At the same time this is a realist cinema that demonstrates a keen eye for detail, for both the modern world and the historical.

The cinema is a phantasmagoria that enables viewers far removed in space and time to experience something similar to that of the original viewers. But the experience will never be the same. For viewers coming to classical Japanese cinema for the first time, or for those who have seen it only as an art cinema, this book is designed to help frame the experience of some of the great works of world cinema within modern Japanese culture. As the memory of this period fades and the films become older, their value as "classics" increases in inverse proportion. It seems more important than ever to shed new light on Japanese cinema of the studio era, to help keep it alive. These films were produced during one of the most turbulent times of world history in a cultural setting that was in a constant state of flux, and in a nation that was becoming modern and "Japanese" within a global media culture.

*Chapter One*

# The Classical, the Modern and Japanese Cinema in the Global System

J apanese cinema has often been thought of as an "other" to Hollywood classical cinema, exhibiting a stylistic alternative to the narrative realism associated with the American industry.[1] The few great directors on whom this assessment is based, however, represent only a tiny fraction of an industry that produced hundreds of films a year for over 30 years. The achievements of Ozu, Mizoguchi and Kurosawa would not have been possible without an established commercial studio system. From 1925 to 1965, Japanese films played on the majority of Japanese screens in thousands of theaters,[2] providing domestically produced entertainment for a nation that fed hungrily on a roster of stars, directors, studios and genres. Filmgoing became part of everyday life in urban Japan in the late 1920s and early 1930s, and with a downturn in production during the war (but not a break), it continued through to the introduction of television in the late 1950s.

Once we consider this era of Japanese cinema as its classical phase, it inevitably entails a coextensive rethinking of the term, and a decentralization of global cinema. Classical Japanese cinema designates another structure of cultural imperialism, and another discourse of modernity, which became a dominant form of mass culture in the twentieth century. The influence of Japanese

1

film on neighboring Asian nations remains largely undocumented (or, more accurately, under-researched). However, even if the distribution of Japanese cinema outside Japan was quite limited during the classical period itself, it has become an important reference point for Japan's former colonies and present trading partners in the region. Given that many films have had second lives on broadcast television, the larger Asian audience for Japanese cinema could be vast, and it arguably continues to grow with the renewed dissemination of films in DVD formats.

Film studies scholars are beginning to question the legitimacy and significance of the "classical" in the American context.[3] In particular, Miriam Hansen's reconceptualization of Hollywood as a form of vernacular modernism,[4] along with Christine Gledhill's and Linda Williams's rethinking of melodrama,[5] have shifted the terms of reference for classical Hollywood cinema from style to culture. These new methodologies have made it possible to consider Japanese cinema of the studio era as a parallel form of classicism. In this chapter, I would like to sketch the larger framework for consideration of modern Japanese cinema as a cultural production in terms of vernacular modernism and melodrama. Although there is a rich tradition of film study in Japan, little of it has been translated. Thus, the discourse on Japanese film in English has been largely framed from outside and, until recently, in markedly Orientalist terms. Recent work by Mitsuyo Wada-Marciano, Aaron Gerow, Peter High, Tom Lamarre and Mitsuhiro Yoshimoto has been instrumental in situating classical Japanese cinema within a more historical and geopolitical framework, augmenting art-historical methods with more sociopolitical approaches to cinema as a cultural practice.

As Eric Cazdyn has noted, the writing of Japanese film history has invariably entailed an implicit construction of a national discourse. If film historians are responsible for producing their objects of study — creating canons, pantheons and critical frameworks — they are also responsible for shaping the communities and social contexts in which films become meaningful.[6] Cazdyn argues for a rethinking of Japanese cinema within a global, transnational context:

> As the global system reconfigures and the contradiction between the national and the transnational comes into greater relief, connections between Japanese film and the world will appear less as esoteric deviations than as the passkeys that allow entrance to a whole new series of productive questions and problems.[7]

Japanese cinema is another global cinema that was produced in the middle decades of the last century, but continues to evolve in the transnational context of its afterlife. Modernity has tended to be perceived as a phenomenon emanating from "the West," and yet the construction of the myth of the West is endemic to modernity itself. In Naoki Sakai's critique of this "emanation model" of modernity, he points out that "[m]odernity is inconceivable unless there are occasions when many regions, many people, many industries, and many polities are in contact with one another despite geographic, cultural and social distance."[8] For Sakai, the key element of cultural heterogeneity in modernity entails that modernity "cannot be considered unless in reference to translation."[9] One way of thinking about classical Japanese cinema is as a translation of the Hollywood idiom into the Japanese vernacular, which is then translated again, with subtitles, to the rest of the world. While this might be fairly obvious in the case of specific directors, I am proposing that it is also true of the institutional context in which these directors worked. The constellation of genres, stars, aesthetics, technologies and personnel that define this cinema constitute a discourse of modernity that reconfigured the national Japanese subject within a global system of representation.

## VERNACULAR MODERNISM

For Miriam Hansen, "classical cinema" is a "technical term that has played a crucial part in the formation of cinema studies as an academic discipline."[10] While popular cinema has tended to be opposed to "modernism," Hansen points out that cinema has played a fundamental role in the historical formation of modernity. Hollywood, in this reading, becomes a key component for the emerging mass publics in the "modernizing capitals of the world."[11] Vernacular modernism incorporates the various cultural practices by which the experience of modernity has been articulated and modified, placing cinema alongside the "everyday" discourses and practices that it also mediates: fashion, architecture, advertising, and so on. In this, Hansen endorses and follows up on Walter Benjamin's key insight that "artistic practices" need to be situated within "a larger history and economy of sense perception . . . the decisive battle-ground for the meaning and fate of modernity."[12] The paradigms of Orientalism have tended to emphasize the Japaneseness of Japanese cinema at the expense of its modernity. The framework of vernacular modernism, however, enables us to move beyond the binaries of East and West to recognize the modernity of this cinema as a discourse of mass culture. The aesthetic and sensual qualities that gave rise to an auteur cinema can be linked more directly to the changing structures of Japanese society, including its paradigms of class and gender.

The precise beginning and end points of classical Japanese cinema are debatable. One might say that this "classical" studio-era cinema evolved in Japan with the establishment of Shochiku film studio in 1920, or we can date it from the experimental phase of the late 1920s in which the scriptwriting advocates of "pure cinema" wrestled filmmaking away from those who had more theatrical stakes in the medium.[13] Aaron Gerow has discussed the discursive context of the Pure Film movement in terms of Japanese modernity as a contradictory and contested social formation. Reformers arguing for the banishment of female impersonators and *benshi*, and pushing for a more "modern" film language, were at once influenced by foreign cinema and eager to promote a more specifically Japanese film style. The discourse of reform in the 1920s was not simply about film production, however. Gerow shows how "there was a supposition of a mass, homogenized audience," and a need aided by institutions of censorship, to train audiences to participate in a "rationalized, urban, modernity."[14]

The establishment and development of classical Japanese cinema in prewar Japan was inextricable from the role of state authority, culminating in the Film Law that was passed in 1939, designed to control film production during the war. But, as early as 1917, it is evident that the discursive context of Japanese cinema underlined its role in the construction of the modern Japanese subject. According to Gerow:

> If Western modernism needed others (the East, the South) to define itself, so did this modernism of purity, only its others were located as much in Japan as in the colonies, if not also in the Japanese text and the Japanese subject. Modernism, in this case, was not a state to be achieved, but a seemingly self-perpetuating process.[15]

The beginnings of classical cinema could also be traced to the drawn-out transition to sound in the early 1930s, especially as it coincided with the beginning of the China-Japan war. It was during this period that many small, independent production companies floundered, and the industry became more streamlined and consolidated around three big companies: Nikkatsu, Shochiku and Toho. The hybridity and stylistic excess that characterized the silent period of Japanese cinema was slowly eliminated and the overall pace of film style slowed down, as prestige works became what one critic has described as "monumental."[16] By 1937 Toho had absorbed Photo Chemical Laboratories (PCL) to become a full-fledged production house, rivaling Shochiku and Nikkatsu, and by the end of the decade it dominated the Japanese industry. Toho, along with the rest of the industry during the 15 years of war, came under the direct control of the imperial government. Nevertheless, the range of filmmaking styles that were produced during the era, including spy films, women's films and family melodramas, alongside the more well-known war films and period films, is surprisingly varied.

Japanese imperial cinema was exported to Taiwan, Korea, China and the Philippines, and after 1937 was also produced in Korea and Manchuria. The propaganda of Japanese colonialism inevitably met with resistance, and produced an increased antagonism among Asian audiences, but, as Sharon Hayashi argues, the framework of imperial oppression and colonial resistance is too simplistic, and cannot account for the full complexity of this transnational cinematic geography.[17] This was the first time many filmmakers traveled overseas, and, in conjunction with the introduction of sound, during the 1930s the cinema solidified around a standardized language, which became necessary for both domestic and overseas audiences.[18]

Hayashi has shown how traveling filmmakers helped to accommodate the diverse regions and dialects of Japan into a national culture through the imagery of landscape made possible in cinematic representation. The urbanism of Japanese modernity was augmented and expanded during the war years with an increased attention to the populations and landscapes of the countryside. Hayashi's research impels us to consider the deep-seated contradictions of this era, manifested in an industrial cinema that was definitely harnessed to the imperial mandate but that was, nevertheless, mobile and decentered. The contradictions of tradition and modernity became enmeshed with the added contradiction of the expanding geographical borders of colonialism. The director Hiroshi Shimizu, for example, produced a series of "road movies" that, Hayashi points out, "were part of the great structural changes in first domestic and then colonial travel and transportation taking place in society and are very much implicated in the colonial project."[19]

Shimizu, like Naruse, has tended to be overlooked by film historians outside Japan because he was not considered "Japanese" enough to represent a national cinema.[20] He made an incredible 163 films over the course of his career and, like Naruse, developed an idiosyncratic style from a hybrid of Japanese and other sources. Shimizu's film practice took him to many different regions of the country and the colonies, and his films include portrayals of Korean communities in Japan, as well as the various social outcasts, migrants and itinerants who live "on the road," beyond and outside the norms of urban society. A renewed approach to Japanese cinema that is better able to grasp its mobility and diversity is urgently needed before more directors such as Shimizu become lost to historical amnesia. Transnational cinema in this sense points to the porosity of a national culture; classicism denotes the integrity of stylistic and industrial characteristics by which we can group these films together.

Many of the key directors of the studio system — including Heinosuke Gosho, Teinosuke Kinugasa, Daisuke Ito, Masahiro Makino, Kenji Mizoguchi, Mikio Naruse, Yasujiro Ozu, Yasujiro Shimazu, Hiroshi Shimizu and Kajiro Yamamoto — began their careers in the late 1920s. In the hierarchical structure of the Japanese studio system, directors beget other directors through apprenticeships as assistant directors and scriptwriters. The late 1920s saw the establishment of key genres including the swordplay films (*chambara*) that became the main genre of period films (*jidai-geki*) and the home drama (*shoshimin-eiga*) that became a key form of contemporary drama (*gendai-geki*). The legacy of the directors and producers of the late silent period lasted well into the 1970s, as many of the generic formulas, including the samurai film and the home drama, were adapted as popular TV genres. Moreover, many directors — including Naruse, Gosho, Ichikawa and Kinoshita — actually outlasted the collapse of the industry and continued to work through the 1960s and 1970s.

The end point of the classical period is likewise subject to debate. The New Wave cinema had many key precedents in the 1950s and did not come out of nowhere. Seijun Suzuki, Yasuzo Masumura, Shohei Imamura and Kaneto Shindo all began their careers in the mid-1950s. And yet, the directors associated with the New Wave in the 1960s condemned the cinema of their predecessors and vowed to challenge what they saw as its staid aesthetics and repetitive formulas. The radical new aesthetics spearheaded by Nagisa Oshima confirm the designation of the cinema that came before as "classical." Many of the new directors produced their films outside the studio system, and began to screen their films alongside the new "independent" cinemas of Europe and America. Insofar as the film industry turned more and more to pink (porno) films, and audiences turned more to TV, the critical rejection of classical Japanese cinema was accompanied by a diversification and fragmentation of the Japanese industry and its audiences.

While it may be difficult to pinpoint precise dates for the rise and fall of classical Japanese cinema, the constellation of changes around 1930 and 1960 leave little doubt that the volume of films produced by the industry through the middle decades of the twentieth century was accompanied by a coherency and stability that is historically circumscribed. To describe the Japanese cinema of the 1930s, 1940s and 1950s as a "classical cinema" is a means of recognizing its integrity as a mode of production that is unlike the cinema that preceded it and unlike that which followed. If classical Hollywood cinema can be described as a national cinema,[21] it is not unreasonable to identify other national examples of industry-based commercial cinemas in countries such as China and India as classical cinemas that built on the model of the American "system" to develop indigenous modern mass cultures.

Anderson and Richie's *The Japanese Film: Art and Industry* (1982) goes a long way toward outlining the contours of classical Japanese cinema, as does the work of Tanaka Junichiro and Tadao Sato, but, as Eric Cazdyn notes, these histories are ultimately unable to let go of the "great man" theory of culture.[22] Even if the Japanese studio system is built around directors, the films themselves are deeply embedded in the culture of modern Japan. The conception of classical cinema that we need to pursue in the case of Japan is the cinema of the everyday, based largely in adaptations of Japanese novels and stories, and constructed from the architectures, fashions, musical idioms and material culture of twentieth-century Japan. The *jidai-geki* likewise consists of the retelling of familiar stories with new personalities and variations over time.

The model of classical cinema that I am proposing is not aligned with the Bordwell, Staiger and Thompson model, although it is certainly influenced by many of the stylistic norms that they identify. A degree of stylistic consistency persists in the classical Japanese cinema but, like its Hollywood counterpart, it was also characterized by contradiction, inconsistency and unevenness — tendencies that the Bordwell, Staiger and Thompson model cannot account for.[23] Rather than a classicism of norms, paradigms and systems, the classical Japanese cinema is built on principles of "decorum, proportion, formal harmony, respect for tradition, mimesis, self-effacing craftsmanship," which Bordwell concedes are also at the basis of Hollywood's classicism.[24] This was basically what André Bazin meant when he designated the American studio system as a classical cinema,[25] and it is through these principles that Japanese filmmakers forged the terms of representation of a modern Japanese culture.

The prewar and postwar "golden ages" of Japanese cinema were produced within historical eras of deep ideological tensions that were only cursorily smoothed over during the 15-year war. Many industry personnel, including Naruse, switched remarkably smoothly in 1946 from making films supporting the war to films supporting revolutionary democracy. The ability to absorb and reproduce competing ideological mandates is at once the condition of classical Japanese cinema and an important and distinguishing feature of it. It should be evident that as an industrial product, from the 1930s until the early 1960s, certain continuities remained in place that allowed Japanese cinema to play a vital role in nation-building, even while the nation endured a dramatic series of ideological upheavals. Harry Harootunian notes that the cinema of the 1930s

> must be situated within a framework marked by unevenness, which Japanese during
> the interwar period were living and experiencing intensely at the most fundamental
> levels of an everyday life constantly crisscrossed by different temporalities and politi-
> cal, economic, social and cultural intensities.[26]

Between 1935 and 1937, while Naruse was at PCL, the mounting escalation of military activities remains entirely unacknowledged in his film practice. Instead, the tensions of everyday life are played out in terms of an idiom of modernity — the cinema — and in terms of rituals and practices that are neither strictly modern nor "traditional." The older customs that persist in this cinema are not always the theatrical and literary arts of high culture but, rather, those of popular song, itinerant actors and the conventions of middlebrow *shimpa* theater. Rethinking this history in terms of vernacular modernism is an important means of accounting for the complexity of national and international pressures on a cinematic practice that continued virtually uninterrupted during the 15 years of war.

Among the signs of a classical cinema is a well-developed star system. A surprisingly small contingent of actors made a great number of films, often making up to ten films a year.[27] The films therefore tend to have an aspect of familiarity, not only due to stylistic and generic repetition but also because they are populated by the familiar faces of character actors and stars, many of whom acted from youth to old age. For example, in one of the last manifestations of the classical cinema, the long-running Tora-san series (*Otoko wa Tsuraiyo* [*It's Tough Being a Man*, 1969–95]), one finds actors such as Chishu Ryu — a mainstay of Ozu's casts — living out their days on the big screen. I would not be surprised if this were also true of other technical and artistic personnel employed by the studios. The stylistic and aesthetic continuities within classical Japanese cinema are partially due to the economies of scale built into the system.

The repetitions of genre and of performers, and the recurring styles of costume and architecture, contribute to the development of what Hansen describes, in the context of Shanghai cinema, as an "idiom of its own kind, a locally and culturally specific aesthetics."[28] Japanese cinema, like Chinese cinema in the mid-twentieth century, addressed nations in crisis, and necessarily negotiated a range of conflicting identities and values, including city-country issues, gender issues and codes of costume, everyday life and social behaviors. The films that Naruse, Shimizu and many other directors made through the 1930s and 1940s constitute an idiom of vernacular modernism that was sustained alongside and somewhat below the purview of the intellectual and political discourses on modernity that dominated the period in Japan. Likewise, the genre films that Naruse made during the Occupation display an awkward and ambivalent grasp of the principles of revolutionary democracy. Indeed, the films of the entire studio period are all open to creative readings in which the ideological contradictions of the era are laid bare.

Classical Japanese cinema may have been inspired by the Hollywood model, but the institutionalized production methods were specific to Japanese social customs. Recent documentaries on Ozu and Mizoguchi released in English, along with memoirs of such people as Teruyo Nogami (Kurosawa's script supervisor) have illustrated these relations in ethnographic detail.[29] Certain rituals of drinking, from which women tended to be excluded, often accompanied the preparation of scripts and the planning of shoots. Hierarchies of personnel tended to be associated with key directors and producers, and employees were organized into *kumi* or crews, who learned the idiosyncratic working methods of directors. Studio employees were not paid anything like their American counterparts, even after the organization of labor after the war; and production methods were in general far less high-tech.

Despite these fundamental differences in the mode of production, on the level of style, narrative and emotional effect, the films produced within the Japanese system were reliable commercial commodities. Even so, as narrative fictions, they do not always conform to the stylistic norms of Hollywood classical cinema, which is why Japanese cinema has tended to be regarded as one of Hollywood's "others." Hollywood classical cinema has been theorized according to a specific set of editing and narrative conventions, which were only partially adopted in classical Japanese cinema. The most well-known auteurs are those who thwarted this system in favor of more expressive techniques and styles; and, across the board, editing conventions did not systematically adhere to the norms of continuity editing. And yet filmmakers evidently developed a cinematic style that had great mass appeal. The model of narrative realism that was associated with psychoanalytic film theory in the 1970s has little real relevance to the aesthetic style of classical Japanese cinema — despite the fact that this cinema was in many ways influenced by and modeled on the American style.

## MELODRAMA

Classical Japanese cinema conforms to neither the "classic realist text" of the apparatus theorists nor the normative style described by David Bordwell. Instead, theories of melodrama offer a more appropriate model for the narrative style that Japanese cinema shared with Hollywood, as well as with other Asian cinemas. As Linda Williams explains, many critics who have challenged the hegemony of the notion of classical cinema have nevertheless retained it as a means of referring to the mass-cultural "mainstream" aspect of moving pictures, with the important caveat that it be reconfigured as a modality of melodrama.[30] Comedy, romance, realism and the infinity of genres that are subsumed within the rubric of the "classical" can also be understood as varieties of melodrama:

the popular form specific to the experience of modern life.[31]

Why should this not also be the case with Japanese cinema? Like American cinema, it evolved to meet the needs of what Williams describes as a "modern, rationalist, democratic, capitalist, industrial, and now post-industrial society seeking moral legibility under new conditions of moral ambiguity."[32] Film scholars' preoccupation with the realist novel has downplayed the equally important role of theatrical melodrama as a nineteenth-century antecedent of the cinema. Recognition of this dimension enables us to locate Japanese cinema in relation to popular Japanese theatrical forms such as *shimpa* and *chambara*. In conjunction with the realist impulse, these melodramatic forms are put into the service of "moral legibility,"[33] which in every cultural setting frequently concerns the plight of women in patriarchy.

Kenji Mizoguchi has long been recognized as a melodramatist, with his highly emotional narratives set in sensuous, stylized, landscapes and sets. The films of many other directors, including Naruse, Ozu and Kurosawa, can also be described as melodramas, once that term is understood as a mode of modernism. Melodrama need not be set in an exotic faraway past, need not be "excessive" and need not be about women. Although these are often characteristic of melodrama, the term can more simply refer to a cinema of expression through which social, moral and historical conflicts are given dramatic form. Like the melodramatic theater of the nineteenth-century French stage, classical Japanese cinema developed a language for a new — bourgeois — social formation. In the early 1930s the Japanese middle class was tempted by the phantasmagorias of consumer capitalism. With the rise of cultural nationalism in the late 1930s, as Japan became more and more distanced from the epicenter of mass culture, we see a huge shift in the detail of material culture. With the Occupation, a *mise en scène* of consumer decadence came to dominate domestic screens with a new erotic dimension.

As an expressive style, melodrama is appropriate to the representation of emotions, cathartic climactic scenes and depictions of the "moral occult" of virtuous characters. If many of these conventions are similar to those of Hollywood films, many are also to be found in the Japanese theatrical traditions of *shimpa*, *bunraku* and *kabuki*. They should not be simply dismissed as American imitations. And yet, to the extent that Japanese directors were influenced by Hollywood and its genres, including westerns, gangster films, women's films and comedies, they inhabited this cinema as the language of modernity. With its ability to accommodate the fluctuating discourses of fashion and technologies characteristic of urban modernity, the cinema is an important cultural space for the translation of everyday life into narrative form.

Peter Brooks's definition of melodrama as "a drama of articulation, a drama that has as its true stakes the recognition and triumph of the sign of virtue,"[34] is true both of Japanese *gendai-geki* and *jidai-geki*. In both "genres," psychological dramas are played out against a *mise en scène* of visual detail, accompanied by soundtracks of musical accents highlighting the emotional trajectory of their struggles — which are often struggles with the characters' own gendered identities as men and women. What is it to be a real man or a real woman in a fallen world? Whether that fall is set in the premodern or modern era, the question is not unlike those posed by western heroes (that is, cowboys) and melodramatic heroines. The strength of the films is often bound up with the "sensual" quality of this expressionistic detail, which accentuates the stakes of the characters' dilemmas. Japanese directors were forging an audiovisual language for a society undergoing rapid and often contradictory cultural shifts. In many ways, the cinema provides a continuity, even a stable discourse, throughout 30 years of social upheaval.

The distinction between *gendai-geki* and *jidai-geki*, which constitutes the genre system of Japanese cinema, corresponds to two modes of melodrama. Mitsuhiro Yoshimoto has made this argument, pointing out that the historical films of *jidai-geki* — which are almost always set in the Edo period — were institutionalized as a genre of mass entertainment spectacle. Yoshimoto points out that the distinction between *jidai-geki* and *gendai-geki* "is a symbolic translation of the larger historical framework within which the issues of modernity, imperialism, and colonialism intersect."[35] He suggests that the melodramatic world of Japanese cinema can be classified into three types of narrative: conflict between individuals and social constraints, the dilemma of social mobility, and the power of the inevitable.[36] While these types are frequently combined, the former two became predominant after the war, while the latter was perhaps more prevalent in prewar cinema.

Yoshimoto's last category, "the power of the inevitable," corresponds to the tendency film of the 1930s (a subgenre of *gendai-geki* showing up social tendencies of inequality), and also to the "typically Japanese" sentiment of *mono no aware*, the feeling of "sweet sadness" provoked by the inevitabilities of nature, mortality, history or social change. Melodrama is a meta-genre through which such aesthetics are dramatized within the terms of contemporary life, or, in the case of the *jidai-geki*, the spectacle of the past. Christine Gledhill describes melodrama as a genre-producing machine that effectively appropriates the materials of folk and urban cultures and combines them with what she calls "more formally coherent traditions" deriving from "an increasingly influential middle-class fiction and theatre of sentimental drama and comedy."[37]

A common view of melodrama is that it is "opposed" to realist styles; it is the feminized, sensual other to more masculine, formal, "classical" styles. But such oppositions cannot be sustained through the cinemas of Italy, Japan, America, India or just about anywhere else, as what is often claimed to be a realist national cinema is almost always also melodramatic. Gledhill argues, "the attempt to define mainstream films as classic neglects not only cinema's melodramatic legacy via the genre system it finds at hand but flies in the face of the beginnings of modernity both in the melodrama machine and in the Bakhtinian novel."[38] Reconfiguring "the classical" not as a formal category but as a discourse of modernity is a means of recognizing the heterogeneity and aesthetic qualities of an industrialized mode of popular culture produced within a specific geohistorical framework.

In the Asian context, cinematic melodrama is frequently a vehicle for staging a conflict between feudal and democratic social values. "The Feudal Family Romance," as M. Madhava Prasad describes it in the context of Hindi film, is a narrative mode in which class struggle, sexual and social relations, and the rights of the individual are played out. Prasad also advocates a more dialectical understanding of the relationship between melodrama and realism, pointing out that melodrama is the modernist response to "a desacralized social order where the free individual is the elementary unit."[39] This is precisely how Peter Brooks theorized the emergence of French theatrical melodrama: as a specific response to a cultural inversion of values in which a new moral order, that of the secular middle class, was played out. In Prasad's analysis, Hindi melodrama is fundamentally linked to the aesthetic realism by which the nation represents itself to itself; and yet it has a very particular configuration of the gaze. If realism entails the "invisibility" of a metalanguage, it is also an aesthetic construction of verisimilitude. In the Hindi cinema, Prasad discovers an "absolutist gaze" embedded in film melodrama: "The gaze is mobilized according to the rules of a hierarchical despotic public spectacle in which the political subjects witness and legitimize the splendor of the ruling class." Prasad indicates how the melodramatic mode of Hindi cinema, as a discourse of modernity, is a site of struggle for an "individualized point of view."[40]

Returning to the question of classical Japanese cinema as a melodramatic modality, we might describe the decentered gaze as one of its defining features. The "realist" styles of its most famous avatars — Ozu, Mizoguchi and Kurosawa — can all be described as formal strategies of decentering the gaze through their respective signatures of idiosyncratic editing, camera movement and narrative structure. With their casual use of continuity editing, Japanese filmmakers of the studio era designed textual strategies of narrative verisimilitude that are not necessarily focalized around a single character's point of view.

The shot-reverse-shot structure of classical Hollywood cinema, upon which psychoanalytic theories of narrative realism were developed by "apparatus" theorists in the 1970s, is not nearly as prominent a figure in classical Japanese cinema. It is used by Japanese filmmakers, certainly, but it is not relied on for effects of character identification. Starting in the late 1950s, many films were shot in widescreen formats, a style that does not lend itself easily to the reverse-shot technique, favoring two shots and tableaux instead. The fact that so many directors used the new aspect ratio with such flair is indicative of how little they needed the reverse shot to create empathetic narratives.

In the postwar period, the strong individual protagonist was undoubtedly an important part of classical Japanese cinema, especially in films by Kurosawa and the war films discussed in Chapter Six. Naruse created many strong female characters over the course of his career, played by actresses such as Setsuko Hara, Hideko Takamine, Haruko Sugimura, Kinuyo Tanaka, Isuzu Yamada and Yoko Tsukasa. These characters may call forth strong identification, yet his melodramatic style was also very observational, ethnographic and distanced. Many of Naruse's women's films end with one or two women walking down a street, over a bridge or down a path. This is a form of closure that leaves something open, some possibility for hope that lies within the companionship of women, the openness of space and the directionality of movement. Ozu's films, like Naruse's, are littered with the signs of social and historical transformation, and both directors tend toward open-ended narratives that do not necessarily adhere to the classical conventions of narrative closure. Ozu's tales of death and marriage such as *Late Spring* (1949) and *Tokyo Story* (1953) partake of a melodramatic mode that dramatizes the dissolution of the traditional household in modern Japanese society. Classical Japanese cinema is characterized by ambivalence and openness, as it eschews the subject-centered gaze of Hollywood for an aesthetic that has often been confused with modernism, but is more accurately understood as the melodrama of modernity.

Gledhill describes the "modality" of melodrama as a mechanism of double articulation, "capable of generating specific and distinctively generic formulae in particular historical conjunctures."[41] The use of realist detail in domestic melodrama anchors the story to a time and place, which in turn renders the narrative as a commentary on that historically specific milieu. In keeping with Sakai's theory of cultural translation, melodrama translates particular aesthetic and narrative struggles and contradictions into popular entertainment. In the postwar period, particularly after the international success of *Rashomon* (1950) in 1951, Japanese films were exported to Hong Kong, Taiwan and Southeast Asia.[42] Kinnia Yau Shuk-ting argues that Japanese samurai films and *chambara* were extremely influential in the development of Hong Kong action films. She also reminds us that, through such projects as Sergio Leone's remake of *Yojimbo* (1961), Japanese cinema in the 1960s had a significant impact on global cinema.[43]

The specific trajectories and networks of influence of Japanese cinema internationally and regionally may be impossible to map in any definitive way. Given the dynamics of melodrama in what we are calling "classical Japanese cinema," however, it may be fair to say that the influence of Japanese cinema in its former colonies may be more complex and far more wide-ranging than official national film histories have thus far admitted. Because melodrama is fundamentally a dramatization of social inequities that are never resolved, its double articulation enables a plethora of readings and receptions.

## CLASSICAL JAPANESE CINEMA AS A TRANSNATIONAL CINEMA

Classical Japanese cinema may be fully legible only in its afterlife as a vehicle of nostalgia and historical imagination. It is in this sense that it becomes transnational, as a theme within what Rob Wilson describes as the "lyric poetry" of the transnational. It has become uncanny and unstable in its new contexts of reception — international cinematheques, television broadcasts and home video — and its construction of a national subject is dramatically removed from contemporary Japanese identities. Wilson argues for a "spectral critique" that might decenter global–local dichotomies alongside American-centric versions of globalization.[44] Hollywood is not, in fact, the "only global cinema" as David Bordwell believes,[45] because Japanese cinema is arguably one of several Asian cinemas that is globally configured as a discourse of modernity. Its uncanny status as a "classical cinema" is precisely due to the fact that it returns as the repressed memory of a particular story of twentieth-century modernity in which imperialism, nationalism, colonialism, capitalism, class and gender can be reviewed and reassessed in sensual narrative form.

To describe this cinema as a "classical cinema" is a means of acknowledging its role in the formation of a modern culture. Film studies scholars have attempted to discipline the Hollywood output into a systematic set of norms (Bordwell, Staiger and Thompson), and into an ideological program (apparatus theorists); while these attempts certainly helped to ground film studies in a disciplinary formation, neither theory is without significant problems. Once we have stripped away the formal characteristics that have been attached to the term "classical" in the American context, it becomes evident that it is primarily the studio infrastructure to which the term applies. The sheer volume of films that look somewhat alike created a dominant aesthetic that in the case of Hollywood had indubitable global influence.

The Japanese studio system, attached as it was to a modernizing imperial culture and bearing the traces also of imperial collapse, constitutes a "classicism" that is in many ways more relevant to the Asian context. The shared cultural territory remains largely unexplored, although we know, for example, that Japanese *shimpa* theater was a key influence on twentieth-century Korean popular narratives;[46] that Taiwanese directors Hou Hsiao-Hsien and Edward Yang were deeply influenced by Ozu; and that the sentimental melodramas of Charlie Chaplin and the women's action films of Pearl White were popular in Japan, Korea and China. Hye Seung Chung suggests how Japanese film magazines helped identify a canon of American films that had particular appeal in Korea, and this kind of discussion has only just begun.[47]

Rethinking classical cinema as a form of vernacular modernism is a means of recognizing the detail and sensuality of material culture and the emergence of new subjectivities within the homogeneity of a visual style. I have tentatively sketched this style in its Japanese incarnation in terms of a decentered aesthetic in which a form of realism supports the melodramatic modalities of *gendai-geki* and *jidai-geki*. The term "classical" is often used to refer to the period that came before the sex and violence of the New Wave and the pink film. But there still seems to be a real hesitation about recognizing how deep the influences of Hollywood were, how they became integrated into Japanese cultural styles of representation and performance, and what kinds of roles such a cinema might have played in constituting a public sphere. The classicism of Japanese cinema is, in this sense, a means of identifying a cultural focal point against which and through which Asian melodrama might be theorized.

A 1993 anthology, *Melodrama and Asian Cinema*, was an important first step in identifying the significance of melodrama in Japan, China, India, the Philippines and Indonesia.[48] The dominant methodology of that collection fell under the category of "cross-cultural criticism," and most authors (including myself) tended to apprehend melodrama as a theoretical model rather than a possible mode of vernacular modernism. Within a transnational model, local histories of theatrical representation might be seen to cross boundaries, languages and cultures in the terms of cinematic representation and its narrative language. Moreover, as Mitsuhiro Yoshimoto points out, "a certain historical consciousness can always be found at the core of melodrama."[49] Its close affiliation with imperialism no doubt makes classical Japanese cinema a bad object and an uncanny bedfellow for much of the region; and yet it is precisely because of this cultural proximity that it needs to be brought into focus. In South Korea, for example, the term *sinp'a* (from *shimpa*) is still used as a derogatory term to designate old-fashioned melodrama derived from the Japanese theatrical mode that was so influential in the 1920s. The genre still tends to carry a bitter aftertaste of Japanese colonialism for South Korean audiences and critics.[50]

Classical cinema in this formulation is not "opposed" to other practices, whether they be art cinemas, cinemas of excess or those from other cultures. It points to the flexibility of a narrative form that crosses linguistic and other boundaries. In twentieth-century Japan, a "classical cinema" could be harnessed to a national culture and, at the same time, undermine that nationalism by implicitly alluding to a global modern culture of "the movies." While this cinema had a very different historical trajectory than its American counterpart, the establishment and full institutionalization of the studio system of production in the 1930s created a base for what can only be described, in retrospect, as a classical Japanese cinema that lasted into the 1960s, with a legacy that has yet to be fully understood.

*Chapter Two*

# Yasujiro Ozu: A Short History of the Home Drama

Yasujiro Ozu is one of the most studied of Japanese directors. He has been positioned as a radical modernist, a transcendental Zen poet, and as an archconservative nationalist. His cinema is rich enough to sustain all such critiques and more. The Criterion releases discussed here include a wealth of special features that help to fill in the scope of Ozu's international influence, and also clarify some of his working methods. Ozu did not have much education outside the cinema, although he was certainly very well versed in international film culture by the time he started directing in 1927. He started as an assistant cameraman in 1923 and made 53 features before his death in 1963.

All of Ozu's films can be classified as "home dramas," and all are *gendai-geki*, set in the twentieth century. The home drama genre, derived from nineteenth-century *keitai shoshetsu* "domestic novels" and *shimpa* drama, is also known as *shoshimin-eiga* or *shomin-geki*, or "films about ordinary people." The genre had a remarkable run through Japanese film history. After Ozu's death, the genre was sustained until 1995 by the Tora-san series of films starring Kiyoshi Atsumi (*It's Tough Being a Man* [1969–95]). Not only did Ozu's contribution to the genre make it a mainstay of Japanese culture but also his formal stylization of central tropes made the genre canonical in world cinema — a point of reference for filmmakers, historians and theorists of all languages. Although there

**Fig. 1** *Tokyo Story* (Ozu, 1953).

is great variety and substantial shifts in style over the course of his career, Ozu developed a very distinctive and recognizable style. This may be why he is so studied, but it is also true that the critical establishment has focused more on the style than the substance of his films. In fact, the family dynamics of the films, and the changes over the 30 years covered here, provide a remarkable insight into Japanese cultural history. We need to keep in mind that Ozu's cinema did not "reflect" the complex and dynamic society of which he was a part. The films were produced within an industrial, commercial setting, and were undoubtedly partially responsible for some of the ideals and fantasies of that society. Along with many other cineastes of his generation, he cultivated a complicated nostalgia for an idealized Japanese past. One of the legends of Ozu is that his films were not released in the West until the 1970s because they were felt by Japanese distributors to be "too Japanese" for Westerners to understand. Such tales are indicative of the extent to which he captured an ideal of Japanese identity that doesn't quite hold up to scrutiny. Not only can Westerners understand these films, they can be moved by them.

One of the most prominent themes of Ozu's cinema is the question of a daughter's marriage. The home drama is a genre about change — about the inevitability of history, signified by death, marriage, birth, the tensions between generations, the flowing of rivers and the running of trains. The momentum of modernity threatens the stability of the home, and yet, despite the relentless ticking of clocks, the home always seems to remain secure. This is not a cinema of crisis but, rather, of imperceptible emotions. The characters are always active — eating, drinking and chatting — but they never really do anything and nothing ever happens. This is the miracle of Ozu.

To date, Criterion has released 21 Ozu titles, including three Eclipse sets. The following discussion covers eight of those titles, including three documentaries included as special features in the *Tokyo Story* (1953) and *Late Spring* (1949) releases. The films discussed here range from *Tokyo Chorus* (1931) to *An Autumn Afternoon* (1962), so one should get some sense of the historical breadth of his career, although this is but a fraction of the director's total output. For more detailed discussion of Ozu's career, David Bordwell's book is highly recommended for his formal analyses and for his introductory chapters on Ozu's social context; for Ozu's working methods, Donald Richie's book *Ozu* is highly recommended.[1]

## SILENT OZU: FATHERS AND SONS

In 2008 Criterion released a box set of three of Yasujiro Ozu's silent films: *Tokyo Chorus* (1931), *I Was Born, But . . .* (1932) and *Passing Fancy* (1933). Most of his 34 silents, along with those of most of his Japanese colleagues, remain unavailable, making this release something of a landmark moment in film history. These three films offer a glimpse of Ozu's early career and are good examples of the dynamic form of Japanese silent film. They also offer remarkable insight into the social milieu, the anxieties and the challenges facing working and middle-class families during a period of rapid modernization. All three titles placed highly in the annual *Kinema Junpo* top-ten polls, indicating that they were very likely popular as well as critical successes in Japanese theaters. *Tokyo Chorus* placed third in 1931, while both *I Was Born, But . . .* and *Passing Fancy* took top prizes in their production years, and were followed by another first prize in 1934 for the silent film *A Story of Floating Weeds*.

Ozu continued to work in the silent medium well after the introduction of talkies in Japan in 1931, making him one of the last global silent directors. Inspired by American comic directors such as Charlie Chaplin and Harold Lloyd, his cutting style in this period is generally far more continuous and "invisible" than in the postwar films for which he tends to be better known. These films make it plain that he learned and mastered the "rules" of narrative cinema, even while he demonstrates a perpetual playfulness with all the conventions of space, time, framing and montage. The fluidity of the silent films is quite unlike the pictorial rigor of the late films, and yet many keys to his auteurist signature are already readily apparent: the low camera angles, the inserts of objects and locations, the "piecemeal" style of constructing conversations and the playful undermining of spatial expectations.

David Bordwell has meticulously detailed the formal and technical traits of these films.[2] He especially underlines the clever ways in which Ozu's silent films are frequently organized around gag structures that are developed into larger narrative patterns. Often these gags turn on repeated gestures, but they also turn on certain spaces and objects that gain layers of significance through repetition and return. Recurring thematic patterns also run through these films, which are organized around the family, the workplace and the suburban locations around Shochiku's Kamata studios where the films were shot. Behind the auteurist idiosyncrasies, these films were produced within a studio system that was consolidated precisely during the early 1930s.

In fact Ozu's silent film style was central to the establishment of the genre system that underscored the Japanese industry through to the 1960s. It was at Kamata, under the supervision of producer Shiro Kido, that the basic contours of the *shoshimin-eiga* (a.k.a. *shomin-geki*) were laid out. Films about "ordinary people" or the emergent middle class were very central to the project of the construction of Japanese modernity. As this was also the target audience of the film industry, the success of the genre involved the translation of everyday life into the new "modern" medium of cinema, enabling Japanese audiences to visualize themselves as part of global modernity. In her book on this period, Mitsuyo Wada-Marciano shows how Ozu and his colleagues in the industry during these crucial years developed a visual language for the representation of a new modern Japanese culture. Shochiku-Kamata studios became "the center of modern film production and the cultural hub of Japanese modernity itself."[3]

The three films in this collection are especially interesting for their depiction of fatherhood and the challenges faced by workingmen attempting to support their families in a depressed economy. The depression hit Japan along with competing discourses of nationalism and modernization, leaving a new class of white-collar workers somewhat stranded in their newly established nuclear families, quite removed from traditional familial support structures. These three films feature three very different male protagonists who are each caught up within a vast network of social hierarchies and pecking orders, economic crises and family responsibilities. All three films could also be described as satirical comedies as Ozu gently mocks the institutions in which his characters are so caught up.

In *Tokyo Chorus*, Shinji (Tokihiko Okada) is a father of three, working for an insurance company. On the day he and his wife expect a big bonus, he gets fired instead for trying to defend an elderly colleague who has been unjustly fired himself. Shinji's confrontation of the boss is a hilarious Chaplinesque scene and quite an unusual challenge of authority. The slapstick display of pushing and shoving is indicative of just how outrageous such insubordination would be in the Japanese workplace. Despite his college education, Shinji cannot find another job until he runs into his former teacher Omura (Tatsuo Saito) distributing flyers on the street. The teacher runs a small restaurant and convinces Shinji to swallow his pride and work with him promoting the restaurant with flyers and banners (like a "sandwich man" in depression-era America). Shinji's wife, Sugako, is also persuaded to accept their new situation, and she helps to ladle out chicken curry. The plot resolves with a school reunion of Shinji's classmates all toasting their former teacher, and during the meal Omura receives a letter announcing a new job he has found for Shinji teaching English in Tochigi Prefecture. Paternal authority is restored, as has the class status of the protagonist.

In *I Was Born, But . . .* the father, Yoshi (Tatsuo Saito), far from confronting his boss, obsequiously sucks up to him. This is probably the most well known of Ozu's silent films, and it is in many ways the most stylistically and thematically tight of the three in this set. Yoshi's two boys, new to the neighborhood, play out their own scenarios of power and social maneuvering, but while they manage to supplant the local bully, they are ashamed at their father's subordination. The film's climactic scene, when the boys and the adults all watch home movies at the boss's house, is a fascinating moment of reflexive filmmaking, with its multiple levels of spectatorship and cinematic representation. *I Was Born, But . . .* is a remarkable portrait of a salaryman who is made to feel inadequate by his own family. Order is restored in the end, as the boys come to understand the inevitability of social convention and they give their father "permission" to light the boss's cigarette. They retain their power over the boss's young son,

**Fig. 2** *I Was Born, But . . .* (Ozu, 1932).

however, with their fairy-tale rituals of "ninja" authority — signalling him to play dead on cue.

*Passing Fancy* features a single father, played by Takeshi Sakamoto, who is not a salaried worker but a laborer in a brewery. Sakamoto's character, Kihachi, became a recurring figure in Ozu's cinema of the 1930s and is the prototype of Tora-san, Kiyoshi Atsumi's character in the long-running Tora-san film series that sustained Shochiku studio from 1969 to 1995. Sakamoto's Kihachi, a widower with a young son, is a much more full-fledged comic character than the fathers in the other two films discussed here, although the narrative of *Passing Fancy* is less satirical. The film concerns the arrival of a homeless young woman into Kihachi's neighborhood. He finds the woman, Harue, a home in a café run by his lady friend Otome (Choko Iida) and a kind of love triangle develops between Kihachi, Harue and Kihachi's buddy Jiro — a younger man who also lives off Otome's cooking. Eventually, after a series of melodramatic misunderstandings, Harue and Jiro get together.

*Passing Fancy* is brought to life by the antics of Kihachi's son Tomio, played by Tomio Aoki, who also plays the younger son in *I Was Born, But . . .* In the 1932 film, the two boys perform routines of doubleness and automatism, invoking the codes of the machine age into their very performance styles. In *Passing Fancy*, Tomio displays a similar repertoire of stylized poses and gestures, even while his character is one of studious responsibility. The child in this film also comes to realize that his father is not a great man, and accuses him of being an illiterate drunk. Father and son forgive each other, but the boy gorges himself

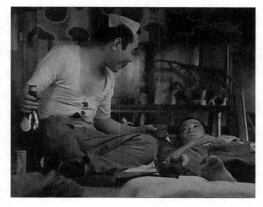

**Fig. 3** Takeshi Sakamoto and Tomio Aoki in *Passing Fancy* (Ozu, 1933).

on candy, almost dies, leaving his father with an impossible doctor's bill. His friends pitch in, and even forgive the debt; but Kihachi insists on traveling to Hokkaido to pay it off. The film ends with him spontaneously jumping ship to return to his son in Tokyo.

*Tokyo Chorus* features a similar incident of a child getting sick from sweets, followed by a huge bill for her father to pay. In that film, Shinji sells his wife's *kimono* (without telling her), which are basically the signature of class inheritance. The way that these films repeat such motifs is indicative of the way the generic formula of storytelling was implanted in the detail of everyday life. The so-called "middle class" was carved from a plethora of new and old social rituals. Children in these films are constantly coveting toys, and of course their parents can never provide enough and thus commodity capitalism is depicted as a kind of eternally unfulfilled desire. Moreover, when Ozu depicts the homes of the wealthy in *I Was Born, But . . .*, decorated with Western furniture, his low-angle camera renders the furniture strangely monstrous. The overindulgence in sweets is symptomatic of the excesses of modern culture that are unevenly and unequally distributed; meanwhile the requisite hospital scenes underscore the science of modern medicine.

Most of Ozu's silent films are examples of the Japanese home drama, although his female characters tend to be far less developed than the men. In both *Tokyo Chorus* and *I Was Born, But . . .* the wives are passive, inexpressive women. Only Choko Iida's Otome, the café owner in *Passing Fancy* is a strong female character, and Iida continued to play supporting and lead roles in Ozu's films into the 1940s. The recurrence of actors in these films and through the entire Japanese industry links them into a larger uber-text of mothers, fathers, widows, bosses, teachers, barkeepers and bar patrons, and vast networks of family members that grew up on screen, playing different generations. Seven-year-old Takamine Hideko, who became a huge star in the 1950s, appears in her first screen role in *Tokyo Chorus*.

One of the recurring sights in these three films is the suburban landscape crossed by telephone poles. The families in both *Tokyo Chorus* and *I Was Born, But...* live in desolate new developments where the houses appear to be cramped yet widely scattered across the empty fields on the outskirts of Tokyo. The empty lots are the terrain where gangs of young boys roam and fathers trudge back and forth from train stations. Factory chimneys mark the horizon and commuter trains slice across the screen. *Passing Fancy* is set in a warren of back alleys, probably close to a suburban train station, and the children in that film also spill out into the empty telephone pole–studded lots. This is in many ways an emblematic landscape of Japanese modernity, a landscape that seems to be waiting for something to happen. But all that happens in these films is that problems are overcome, forgotten or reconciled, and life goes on under sunny skies.

In Ozu's cinematic language, the homes and public spaces take on an aspect of familiarity through repetition, and through his pictorialist framing. Among the most distinctive features of his style in this period are lateral pans over people and objects. In the opening scene of *Passing Fancy*, the camera pans over

**Fig. 4** Tomio Aoki and Hideo Sugawara in *I Was Born, But...* (Ozu, 1932).

an audience watching a show, fanning themselves in the heat. Later in the film a scene opens with a pan over an array of household objects, which we learn Kihachi is hoping to pawn. *Tokyo Chorus* opens with rows of college students performing drills badly, and the clowning around is punctuated by a tracking shot over the line of men. Because Ozu rarely moves the camera, the occasional pans and tracking shots tend to stand out. Moving slowly over the empty desks in Shinji's office in a subsequent scene in *Tokyo Chorus*, the camera movement echoes the previous line of men; now they are lined up for their bonuses outside the boss's door.

The introduction to the insurance office in *Tokyo Chorus* moves over an array of objects — fans, typewriters, messy desks — and is then broken down into discrete close-ups of less businesslike objects: a soda with a straw, a pair of shoes on a desk. These collections of objects, featured in camera pans or in series of shots, exaggerate the everydayness of Ozu's cinema. They underline the way that the characters are constructed through their *mise en scène*: the spaces and objects around them. In each film only one or two actors are more expressive than the décor. The others, including wives, children and fellow workers, are little more than props. Ozu's world is by and large a friendly one, in which the detritus of material culture speaks plainly and openly. His father figures struggle within this world of things to sustain their sense of paternal authority, even while that authority is relentlessly given over to the systems of modernity that lie beyond their grasp.

**Fig. 5** *Tokyo Chorus* (Ozu, 1931).

The Criterion releases are all scored by Donald Sosin, and *I Was Born, But* . . . features a particularly fun ragtime score that complements the *nansensu* (nonsense) elements of Ozu's comedy. The print quality of *Passing Fancy* and *I Was Born But* . . . is fair, but *Tokyo Chorus* is somewhat damaged, although the patina of decay is not terribly obtrusive. *Passing Fancy* is the most burdened of the three films by a plethora of intertitles, almost as if it had been written as a talkie. Nevertheless, Ozu plays with these as well, often leaving the viewer in doubt as to who is speaking — starting with the opening stage performance. All three films open with lovely sequences of stylish flourishes that have tangential bearing on the subsequent stories. In these prologues — a moving truck in *I Was Born, But* . . ., a *naniwa-bushi* variety show in *Passing Fancy*, and the phys-ed college scene in *Tokyo Chorus* — Ozu establishes a comic tone that is embedded in the idiosyncratic detail of everyday life. These prologues with minimal dialogue are each also, in their own way, tributes to the language of silent film that Ozu undoubtedly recognized as a medium on the verge of disappearance.

## *A STORY OF FLOATING WEEDS* AND *FLOATING WEEDS*: OZU REMAKES HIMSELF

*A Story of Floating Weeds* (1934) and the 1959 remake *Floating Weeds* are anomalous in Yasujiro Ozu's oeuvre in that they are set in rural villages where the trappings of modern life are more or less sidelined. Most of the characters wear *kimono* and the action is set in narrow streets that appear somewhat timeless. Despite the fact that these are stories of the twentieth century, the packaging of the DVD features Edo-period woodblock prints of stylized actors' faces, suggestive of a period setting. Ozu is well known to have never made a *jidai-geki* or period film, and while these two versions of *Floating Weeds* may indeed be as close as he came, the packaging is somewhat incongruous. As striking as it may be, the cover art belies a lingering Orientalism on the part of the distributors.

The title, *Floating Weeds*, refers literally to *ukigusa* or duckweeds, and metaphorically to the aimlessness of life's journey. The itinerant acting troupe that the two films are about is emblematic of this trope of Japanese poetics: traveling entertainers who are at once homeless but at home everywhere as they move from one theater to another across the country. Donald Richie refers to their particular brand of theater as "country *kabuki*,"[4] but it is also a variant of *taishu engeki*, a kind of third-rate *kabuki* that is specific to modern Japan. Cultural theorist Marilyn Ivy describes it as an assemblage of song spectacle and "samurai melodrama," along with comedy and dance routines, combined into a vaudeville-like sequence of acts.[5] The brief scenes that Ozu offers of the troupes' performances suggest an entertaining hybrid of low-budget traditional performance styles combined with farce.

**Fig. 6** *A Story of Floating Weeds* (Ozu, 1935).

In the 1930s, when *A Story of Floating Weeds* was made, *taishu engeki* was extremely popular, flourishing alongside the new mass culture of movies and sports. However, because it was performed in the marginalized sites of rural theaters and small variety halls in long-standing urban entertainment districts, it also retained the flavor of the local, and a nostalgia for Edo-period culture. While *kabuki* had been sterilized into a staid traditionalism, *taishu engeki* retained the non-institutional character of a folk culture. *Taishu engeki* is a theater form that belongs to the working and lower middle classes. By 1959, when Ozu remade the story, *taishu engeki* was itself disappearing, and so the later film is doubly nostalgic — for its 1930s popularity and for the Edo-period sources of the theatrical forms. The postwar film is especially ambivalent concerning the class status of this populist theater, as the idealization of the 1930s had given way to a rejection of its cheap and "vulgar" aesthetics. In the 1930s, Ozu may have aspired to bring his cinema close to the popular roots of *taishu engeki*, but 25 years later his cinema is so far removed from that culture that

the central character Komajuro (Ganjiro Nakamura) can express only shame
for his profession.

The co-release of the two films provides a rare opportunity to compare the
prewar and postwar cultural contexts that can be read in each film, despite
the rural settings. It also enables a comparison of Ozu's style in both periods.
Although neither film is necessarily "typical" of the director's treatment of family life, they both exhibit his usual idiosyncratic tendencies, and in this they are
remarkably similar. The 1934 film is said by some critics to mark the beginning
of Ozu's melancholic attitude toward the disintegration of the modern family;
he also refines some of his most consistent formal constructions, such as the low
camera angle and the "pivot object" that recurs to link different shots and scenes
that are otherwise discontinuous. The 1959 film follows the original plot and
storyline fairly closely, with the addition of a few new characters and a comic
subplot. Shot by Kazuo Miyagawa, the cameraman responsible for *Rashomon*
(1950) and *Ugetsu monogatari* (1953), *Floating Weeds* is a stunning example of
color cinematography.

The central plot of both films concerns an actor who brings his troupe to a
small town, where a former mistress lives with her 20-year-old son. (The names
of the characters are different in the two versions, each of which plays their
own little games with name-matching.) The son believes that his father died
when he was young and that the actor is his uncle. The story of patrimonial
revelation/discovery is complicated by the actor's current girlfriend, who is a
member of his troupe. Out of jealousy, she bribes a younger actress to seduce
the son, because she knows it will upset the actor. The whole plot hinges on the
shame attached to the actors' profession as itinerant entertainers: the master
of the troupe wants his illegitimate son to do better than himself in life, which
means disavowing his role as head of the family. Meanwhile, the troupe's show
is canceled due to poor attendance and the actor is forced to disband the group,
confirming the insecurity and vulnerability of his chosen profession. The
story ends with the actor-master leaving the town on a train with his actress-
girlfriend beside him, happily pouring his sake, while the former mistress is left
behind with her fatherless son.

The two versions of the film place the emphasis on slightly different aspects
of the story. In the 1934 version, the former mistress (Choko Iida) evokes more
sympathy, not only because of her expressive acting style but also because there

is a darker tone to the whole picture. While there are a few comic moments
in the film, they are mainly confined to the theatrical performances — such
as a two-man horse costume and a boy in a dog suit. Ozu makes use of some
of the religious iconography of the setting for poetic effects. He also stages a
number of scenes in which actors' movements are carefully synchronized: the
actor and his son fishing, and the two actresses putting on makeup backstage.
But as David Bordwell points out, there is less irony than harmony in these
remarkable scenes. Bordwell is in fact disappointed with the comparatively
little playfulness of this Ozu film compared with the kineticism of some of his
other work from the period.[6] What Bordwell describes as "ideological gravity"
is a kind of moral correctitude of the Japanese "tendency film" that highlights
irreconcilable class divisions.

The piano score on the Criterion DVD, composed by Donald Sosin, is
competent, but is such a predictable and clichéd compendium of motifs of the
romantic repertoire that it has the unfortunate effect of smoothing over those
wonderful tics of Ozu's decoupage — even if the musical style might be close
to Ozu's own sentimental taste in music. Not to be overlooked, though, are the
striking *kimono* and *obi* patterns that the actresses wear (offstage), which we can
be sure Ozu himself would have selected, given his fastidiousness over props
and costumes. Two surprising tracking shots within the space of the theater
are further signs of his ability to bring out the inner poetry of everyday life and
are indicative of his more "flamboyant" 1930s style. Although a mountainous
landscape can occasionally be glimpsed in the background, the director seems
somewhat stylistically lost outside his usual urban setting.

Although the 1959 version has Sugimura Haruko cast as the actor's former
mistress, she is curiously inexpressive, reduced to an automaton whose main
chore is to pour sake for her errant lover. Meanwhile, the father-actor, played
by the *kabuki* performer Ganjiro Nakamura, is extraordinarily large in his
movements. Thus, the emphasis at the end is less on the abandoned family,
and more on the actor who strives to become a better actor and return as a
success. In both versions there is a kind of narrative itinerancy in which "life
goes on" with no guarantee of closure, but in the postwar version, there is more
of a carefree attitude, almost as if the actor is escaping the burdens of family
life at the end of the film. Indeed, the seaside village of the 1959 version offers
even less natural surroundings, and most scenes are set in enclosed spaces or

narrow streets. Even the "love scene" between the actor's son and the younger actress, while spiced up for the late 1950s, is dominated by the huge looming boat hulls of a shipyard.

The art direction and cinematography of *Floating Weeds* is based on a palette of muted blues and grays accented by bright-red details that punctuate every set. Along with the grid-like system of framing typical of Ozu's mature style, the village becomes something of a cage or trap: its beauty is so formalized and stylized that it is oddly drained of life, despite the strategically placed red blossoms. The only relief can be found in the local brothel, where the unemployed actors lounge about, begging drinks from the local ladies. Robert Ebert provides the commentary for this disk, and his suggestion that the prostitute who is incongruously clad only in a slip may be inspired by the recent titillating popularity of *Cat on a Hot Tin Roof* (1958) is entirely plausible. Only, in this case, the woman is designated as the ugly (and older) duckling of the flock. The extra half hour of the 1959 version is in fact mainly devoted to the sexual innuendo of the bored, unemployed actors, and a more extensive treatment of the affair between the actor's son (played rather woodenly by Hiroshi Kawaguchi) and the younger actress (played wonderfully by the rising young star Ayako Wakao).

Partly because Ozu made the 1959 *Floating Weeds* at Daiei studio rather than his usual Shochiku, it is a rather uneven film, and doesn't quite achieve the grace of some of his other work of the period. The change of studio may explain some of the inconsistencies of the performances, as well as the gratuitous light sex comedy that seems somewhat tacked on. However, working at Daiei gave Ozu the opportunity to work not only with cinematographer Miyagawa but also with Daiei's top actress, Machiko Kyo, who plays the actress-mistress Sumiko. One of the real highlights of this film is her performance as a young samurai in the *taishu engeki* stage production. Cross-dressing was common for both men and women in this theater, and Kyo does a great turn, complete with garrulous *kabuki* barking and flamboyant striking of poses. Oddly enough, Ganjiro Nakamura is not seen on stage, although he is briefly seen in full makeup, and his voice can be heard from offstage. Ayako Wakao also performs a wonderful dance routine as a geisha who is mimed by a young boy in the troupe. The audience throws packs of cigarettes onto the stage to express their appreciation for the performances. In these fragments of *taishu engeki*, Ozu manages to capture

**Fig. 7** Machiyo Kyo in *Floating Weeds* (Ozu, 1959).

the flavor of the popular theater; but he also contradicts the narrative premise that this is an unworthy form of drama.

In both versions, the paternalistic master-actor has the habit of slapping people around, especially women. He hits the two actresses when he hears that they have seduced his son; and he hits the son as well, until the son finally hits him back. This is a story about the disintegration of paternal authority, as the son refuses to accept the violent old man, the "floating weed" traveling actor, as his father. In the 1934 version, when the father first sees his son, he says proudly, "he'll be eligible for the draft next year," but in 1959 he wistfully remarks that the boy would have made a good recruit. In 1959, there was no army to join, and the new generation was looking for ways to get out of the shadow of their parents' generation. The son criticizes his father's acting and dismisses the character he plays as "old-fashioned." When the father declares that he will return as a better actor in a better class of theater, he can be doomed only to TV, where *taishu engeki* was briefly revived in the 1980s. In the late 1950s TV was poised to render a popular theater like this obsolete. *Kabuki*, meanwhile, was long since reserved for a handful of highly trained actors of designated lineages.

TV also eventually rendered Ozu's leisurely paced family dramas obsolete, and *Floating Weeds* is in many ways a "late" film, in which the director returns to an old story almost as a stylistic exercise. Like American melodrama of this period, the ideological contradictions are too much for the narrative to bear, and it breaks apart under its own weight. Ozu's prototypical cheery ice cream–truck musical score sounds slightly inane in this film, as it flattens out the melodramatic intensities of sex and violence. The characters are stranded in a cultural abyss in which the contest between first-class *kabuki* and third-rate popular theater seems extraordinarily irrelevant to the generational tensions being played out. Both films are ultimately about the emergence of a middle class, for whom Ozu's cinema and the mass medium of motion pictures provided a new form of entertainment.

## *LATE SPRING*: OZU'S DREAMWORLD

In the context of Yasujiro Ozu's impressive oeuvre, *Late Spring* holds a special place. Sometimes referred to as his "most perfect" work, it seems to crystallize almost all of the director's most cherished themes and stylistic traits. As a kind of pivotal film made during the American Occupation, *Late Spring* lays the groundwork for the ensuing 13 years and 12 films of Ozu's mature period. It provides a template for his distinctive orchestration of the Japanese family, the cinema and everyday life in a form that is at once extraordinarily simple and rigorously refined. The passing of time and the passing of seasons inevitably become allegories for the passing of Japan itself into cosmopolitan modernity, and this film is exemplary of Ozu's melancholia within the pressures of history and social change.

The family of *Late Spring* consists only of a father, a daughter and a meddling aunt. The story concerns the marriage of the daughter, Noriko (Setsuko Hara), a 27-year-old woman in the "late spring" of her life. Her father, Somiya

**Fig. 8** Chishu Ryu and Setsuko Hara in *Late Spring* (Ozu, 1949).

(Chishu Ryu), pretends that he will remarry so that Noriko will be able to leave him without regret, but she agrees to the marriage arranged by her aunt (Haruko Sugimura) reluctantly, with very little joy. These are some of the finest actors in Japanese cinema, and Ozu litters the film with exquisite scenes of traditional Japanese iconography, cultural rituals and arts. The film is famous for its inclusion of tea ceremony, *Noh* drama and the temples and gardens of Kyoto, where Noriko and Somiya travel on their last vacation together. And yet there is something deeply unsettling in the film's negotiation of the values of social propriety, traditionalism and the "new world" of democratic postwar Japan.

Noriko's best friend, Aya (Yumeji Tsukioka), is a secretary who married for love, only to become disappointed and divorced. Somiya's best friend, Taguchi (Hohi Aoki), is a widower who has remarried. In contrast to these "progressive" characters, Noriko is extremely conservative. She finds it extremely distasteful — "indecent," even "filthy" — that Taguchi has remarried, and she tells him so. She eventually confesses to her father that it might be okay for him to remarry, and that she is over her disgust. She makes this confession as they sleep side by side in the dark in a Kyoto inn, during a scene punctuated by cutaways to a softly lit composition of a vase in front of bamboo silhouetted on a paper screen. This famous "vase scene" has sparked a great deal of critical commentary as critics struggle to account for the significance of shots that seem so portent, and yet are so obliquely inserted. They may give shape to Noriko's emotions, but they do not represent her point of view.

Like so many of Ozu's family dramas, *Late Spring* turns on the generational differences of modernity, and also on the gendered fabric of Japanese society. Somiya is one of Ozu's many benevolent, idealized fathers, but here he seems more up to date than his daughter, who lives in a kind of dream world of social stasis. The photo of her fiancé is passed around to everyone but the viewer. We are told repeatedly that he looks like Gary Cooper, but we are never once given a glimpse of his face, and no explanation is given for Noriko's acquiescence to the arranged marriage. Early in the film she goes out with another man, Hattori (Jun Usami), her father's assistant, but when it is revealed that he is engaged already to another woman, Noriko shows no disappointment. Noriko is not without emotions, but she — or perhaps it is Hara, Ozu's emblematic actress — refuses to reveal them. The central conflict is not between the love match and the arranged marriage, but between Noriko's obligation to her father and her obligation to the institution of marriage.

Despite its elegance and beauty, *Late Spring* is extremely frustrating in its obliqueness. The year before the film was released, women's rights were finally enshrined in the Japanese constitution. The character of Aya signals the presence of women's newly gained rights to property and divorce, as Richard Peña notes in his excellent commentary for the film. In this context, Noriko is clearly a woman clinging to the old ways, although she is also a woman who tries without success to have things her own way. Social protocol dictates that she cannot remain a single woman living with her father, and she is literally pushed out of her own home. Not only does Ozu refuse to show the fiancé, he also leaves out the wedding itself. Noriko dressed in her bridal costume, like a living doll, is all that is shown of a marriage based on nothing more than a vague reference to an American movie star.

The new Criterion release of *Late Spring* is accompanied by Wim Wenders's documentary *Tokyo-Ga* (1985), a homage to Ozu that is also a personal meditation on Tokyo, Japanese culture and cinema. For Wenders, Ozu is a "sacred treasure of the cinema" who belongs to a fast-retreating past. Wenders is in awe of his technical and formal rigor, his "economy of means" and his beautiful depiction of melancholia and loss. Wenders offers a brief lesson in cinematography by framing a shot of one of Ozu's emblematic corridor-like street scenes, and then switching the lens to Ozu's preferred 50 mm, instantly flattening the image and reducing the depth of field. In interviews with Chishu Ryu and cinematographer Tatsuo Atsuta, we learn about the director's working methods

**Fig. 9** Setsuko Hara in *Late Spring* (Ozu, 1949).

(and drinking habits) and also about the deep respect these men held for the director who they "served" for large parts of their careers.

Despite Wenders's admiration for Ozu, his own filmmaking style could not be more different in *Tokyo-Ga*. Where Ozu is controlled and precise, Wenders is aleatory, wandering and contingent. Both films are meditative, and Wenders takes long pauses to look at the wonderful sights he finds in 1980s Tokyo, but his framing is far more mobile than Ozu's geometrical designs. On the top of the Tokyo Tower, Werner Herzog complains to Wenders that Tokyo is a "ravaged landscape." He says that "we need images . . . clear transparent images," and suggests that one must be an archeologist to excavate such images from the urban landscape stretched out before them. Wenders's Tokyo nevertheless displays a certain clarity, even if it is inevitably the tourist's view of the city. In any case, it is alive, vibrant, colorful and dynamic. His scenes of fake-food manufacturing (wax models for restaurant window displays), rockabilly dancing in Shibuya, pachinko machines, train travel, roof-top driving ranges and taxi-mounted TVs display the exoticism of everyday life in a chaotic urban metropolis. Wenders may bemoan the total disappearance of Ozu's Tokyo, but his own Tokyo is nevertheless exemplary of "life itself . . . moments of truth."

In Wenders's voice-over monologue, he claims that in Ozu's filmmaking "people revealed themselves as they really are." He reads Ozu as a realist whose honesty in depicting reality "can no longer be found today." This is an odd assessment of Ozu's style, especially given the evidence that Wenders himself presents to the contrary. Ozu's use of the 50 mm lens, for example, distorts reality into a two-dimensional picture plane; meanwhile, the interviewees make it abundantly clear that the director exerted total control over all aspects of every production. Chishu Ryu understood very little about the characters he played, but simply followed Ozu's instructions about how to move and deliver his lines. As a 45-year-old man playing a man in his 60s in *Late Spring*, he certainly wasn't playing "himself." Atsuta notes that Ozu avoided location shooting as much as possible because there was too much contingency and potential for losing control of the production.

*Tokyo-Ga* is bookended by the opening and closing scenes of Ozu's film *Tokyo Story*, complete with opening credits and final coda. Wenders's documentary might be thought of as part of a cycle of films that includes *The State of Things* (1982) featuring Sam Fuller, and *Lightning Over Water* (1980), a paean to the

**Fig. 10** Chishu Ryu in *Tokyo-Ga* (Wenders, 1985).

dying Nick Ray. In all three films, Wenders compares himself with his auteurist forebears, to find himself in a fallen cinema. He longs for a more "classical" era when filmmakers could assume that transparency of realism from which his own generation of auteurs is hopelessly alienated. This terrain was already well traveled by Jean-Luc Godard before Wenders even arrived on the scene, and yet Wenders sustained his own melancholia through the early 1980s (including *Hammett* and *Chambre 666*, both 1982). *Tokyo-Ga* is exemplary of the way that he maps his own auteurist persona onto that of another director. And yet, viewed back to back, or side by side, the contrast between *Tokyo-Ga* and *Late Spring* tends to highlight the fundamental differences between Wenders's documentary-based cinema and Ozu's studio-based style.

One of Ozu's signature traits that Wenders overlooks is his idiosyncratic use of background music. The familiar, jingly ice cream–truck music is key to the sense of lightness that pervades the early scenes of *Late Spring*. However, from the outset, this upbeat rhythm alternates with stately strings that gradually take over the soundtrack. The dynamic contrast between the two musical themes suggests that the lightness was only a façade, behind which there is nothing. Cinema is an illusion, life is an illusion, happiness is an illusion. This is Ozu's cinema of truth. The characters are resigned to their fates; they are merely pawns in a game played by a master of his art. *Late Spring* is a key film in Paul Schrader's assessment of Ozu as a Zen master of the cinema, but such an aesthetic tends to be at the expense — in this film anyway — of self-determination for the characters.

The scene in *Late Spring* in which Hattori invites Noriko to a violin concert, but she declines with a wide enigmatic grin, is typical of Ozu's depiction of emotional tension. This is after the revelation of Hattori's engagement, and the unspoken implication is that he is willing to flaunt the rules, but she most definitely is not — out of respect for his unseen fiancée. Ozu shows us Hattori in the theater audience, but withholds any shot of the concert itself. Instead, he cuts to a low-angle shot of Hattori's hat on the empty seat beside him, pointing to his absent date. The scene concludes with two long shots of Noriko walking along the street, entirely expressionless, disappearing around a corner while the soundtrack segues from the light musical theme to the heavier strings. In Ozu's poetic visual vocabulary, discontinuous objects, figures and spaces compensate for radical elisions and absences. The regret felt by both characters is palpable, and even melodramatic to the extent that the imagery might be said to overcompensate for repressed emotion.

The comparison with *Tokyo-Ga* actually shows up Ozu at his most manipulative. Noriko is conned into a marriage that she may or may not want, but the viewer, too, is led into false assumptions. Noriko's pastoral date with Hattori in which they merrily bicycle to the beach in Kamakura is practically romantic, and we are let down as much as her father to learn that Hattori is already engaged. Ozu's playful compositions in which characters sit side by side, duplicating each other's postures, are cues that they are part of a larger design. Somiya's pretence that he will marry, along with Ozu's startling ellipses, are more narrative tricks that suggest that we should place Ozu alongside Alfred Hitchcock and Fritz Lang as directors who toy with their audiences along with their characters.

**Fig. 11** *Late Spring* (Ozu, 1949).

*Late Spring* concludes with the old man, Somiya, alone at home, having told the biggest lie of his life and paying the price with loneliness. Ozu has led us to believe that he might in fact have been interested in Mrs. Miwa to whom he nods politely at the *Noh* play. The scene at the theater is 7 minutes long, constituting a long pause in the middle of the film, and yet the play is interrupted and even upstaged by Noriko's shock at seeing the momentary exchange of glances between her father and the woman across the room. The traditional arts become a kind of backdrop for the family melodrama, and yet Ozu retreats back into the conventions of Japanese poetry to conclude the film, indulging in the sweet sadness of inevitability, transience and solitude. Among Ozu's skills is an ability to draw on a cosmopolitan cultural economy of style that he can incorporate into the film as he pleases. For example, he may privilege the *Noh* play over the violin concerto on the level of the image, but he fully exploits the emotional potential of strings for his own soundtrack.

Noriko disappears after last being seen in her bridal costume, a woman who is either unwilling or unable to express her desires, sent off to marry a man she has barely met. In the context of Occupation Japan, *Late Spring* depicts a dreamworld of an idealized national culture. Tokyo in 1949 was as dynamic and chaotic as Wenders's version of the mid-1980s, as evidenced in contemporary films such as Kurosawa's *Stray Dog* (1949) and *Scandal* (1950), and Naruse's *The Angry Street* (1950) and *Ginza Cosmetics* (1951). The retreat to the past was undoubtedly a respite from the confusion of the era, and an implicit challenge to the edicts of Occupation censors to emphasize "democratic" themes, but Wenders is naïve to think that Ozu's Japan ever actually existed. It was a fantasy that Ozu skillfully brought to life, but only through a production system based on a rigorous hierarchy of roles.

As Donald Richie notes in his essay included in the Criterion package, Setsuko Hara finally escaped the grand design of Ozu's cinema by retiring from public life in 1961. *Late Spring* is the first in a series of five films in which she returns again and again as the unmarried or widowed daughter or daughter-in-law. It sets the tone of her mythic status as Japan's "eternal virgin," embodying an ideal of purity, asceticism and self-sacrifice within a changing world. While Ozu's distinctive style endows everyday life with an aspect of spirituality, Hara's enigmatic performance conveys the tension of a woman trapped in someone else's dream.

## *TOKYO STORY*: THE DIRECTOR AND THE CITY

Released in 1953, 1 year after the end of the Allied Occupation of Japan, *Tokyo Story* has become the canonical film about the difficult rebirth of modern Japan. The story of aging parents and an emerging generation gap is mapped onto the split between rural and city life symptomatic of modernization. On many levels this is a "universal" story with deep currents of humanist emotion. The complicated relationships between parents and their adult children have rarely been as sensitively handled. And yet, as its title suggests, *Tokyo Story* is also very much about one city at one moment in time, and dwells on a level of historical specificity that is equally crucial to its lasting effects. Ozu's particular means of treating historical change and transition rests on a sense of resignation to the loss of the old ways, and a certain anxiety about what the future holds. At the same time, *Tokyo Story* is exemplary of the director's idiosyncratic use of film style, ironically displaying a mastery of the modern idiom of film language.

Ozu is the master of the story in which "nothing happens," but of course everything happens in such a story. The constellation of values and personalities in *Tokyo Story* play off each other in a meandering narrative that takes its time to circle back to the home in which it begins. The older couple makes the long journey to Tokyo, only to find that their son and daughter are too busy to spend time with them; the couple are disappointed to find their children's homes in cramped suburban neighborhoods. Only Noriko, played by the saintly Setsuko Hara, the daughter-in-law whose husband has died in the war, drops what she's doing to take the elderly couple sightseeing. Noriko's faithfulness to her dead husband saddens the parents, who encourage her to remarry. By the end of the film, in classic Hara form, Noriko may or may not have reluctantly agreed to comply.

Noriko's saintliness is counterbalanced by the shrewish sister Shige, played by the great stage actress Haruko Sugimura. Although Shige cold-heartedly complains about the burden of her parents, and callously claims her inheritance without delay after the mother's death, Sugimura's performance adds an important spark of life to the film. Ozu excels in the crucial comic touch. While his style has been variously described as "transcendental," spiritual and "pure," he himself described his craft as that of a tofu-maker. And in this sense, the details of everyday life, including the vulgar and vernacular elements of Japanese

**Fig. 12**  Chieko Higashiyama and Setsuko Hara in *Tokyo Story* (Ozu, 1953).

modernity, are what animate his cinema. Ozu was a huge fan of American films. The claim that he was the "most Japanese" of Japanese directors is a convenient way of ignoring his appropriation of the breezy style of Hollywood comedy and the dramatic realism of American melodrama. Through his distinctive formal effects of low camera angle, reduced camera movements and geometric framings, he made these genres his own, situating them among the "ordinary people" — primarily the lower middle class — of Japan.

*Tokyo Story* is in many respects a "perfect film" in its internal coherence, its balance and its weight of national allegory. At the same time, it belongs to a larger cycle of films that begins more or less with Ozu's collaboration with scriptwriter Kogo Noda on *Late Spring* in 1949 and continues to his final film, *An Autumn Afternoon*, in 1962. The repetition within this group of films of themes, actors, settings and formal techniques is unparalleled in film history. In this respect, *Tokyo Story* is only one movement of a larger project in which, in some respects, it is anomalous. His repertoire of effects and themes are mapped, more clearly here than anywhere else, onto the historical backdrop of Japan's largest city. This is not just a story set in Tokyo; it is *the* story of postwar Tokyo, a tale of the family of Japan trying to find the way forward after the 20-year turmoil of war and occupation.

One of the trademarks of Ozu's style is his use of the architecture of the Japanese home. His framings, editing devices, camera angles and elimination of camera movement are all predicated on the regular, symmetrical forms of domestic architecture. While *Tokyo Story* exploits these elements for a number of different sets, they are also contrasted with the messy sprawl of the metropolis that is briefly glimpsed and traversed in the old couple's journey. The familial home in Onomichi is set among temple statuary and architecture overlooking a harbor, lending the "hometown" or *furusato* a spiritual dimension that is quite evidently missing from the city. Nevertheless, except for the youngest daughter, Kyoko, the grown children have committed themselves to urban life and have little time to spend in Onomichi, even for their mother's funeral.

**Fig. 13** Chishu Ryu and Chieko Higashiyama in *Tokyo Story* (Ozu, 1953).

David Desser's commentary on the new DVD release does a good job of explaining the idiosyncrasies of Ozu's use of 360-degree space and other flagrant violations of classical editing conventions. *Tokyo Story* is rich with typical Ozu conceits of graphic matching, intermediary spaces and narrative ellipses, although what is truly remarkable is the "flow" that is achieved despite these devices. Indeed, the sense of historical momentum and change is embodied in the very rhythm of the film's editing, along with its opening and closing shots of the river-like Onomichi harbor. Like the trains, boats and water flowing to the sea, the story of Tokyo is a story of relentless transformation. Ozu's real achievement is to have taken the "sweet sadness" of classical Japanese poetry, and applied it to the perception of modernity as an unstoppable train. Ozu's characters are carried along by history, but they will never change it.

The Criterion DVD release retains the "patina" of the celluloid original, along with the hissing and popping of audio flaws. Unfortunately, the subtitles occasionally lapse into white-on-white invisibility despite the fact that they have been revised. The image is not nearly as crisp as the Kurosawa releases by the same company, although in some respects the texture of the old print is rather nice, as it registers the historical specificity of the film's production. The two-disk set contains two valuable additional documentary features, both produced by Shochiku studio, the company Ozu worked for all his life.

The real surprise is the 2-hour 1983 documentary *I Lived, But . . .* by Kazuo Inoue. Tracing the entire trajectory of Ozu's life and career, it transcends the usual hagiographic narrative by including a large selection of clips and interviews with many key collaborators and friends of Ozu's. This is the kind of resource that English-language film scholars have long been lacking, as it provides rare insight into Ozu's working methods and personality. The clips are particularly well chosen, many of them from hard-to-see titles, including silent films such as *Days of Youth* (1929) and the college and Kihachi series of the early 1930s. Employing a full repertoire of experimental and "flamboyant" techniques, and comic acting styles, the dynamism of the early films is a far cry from the static formalism of the "mature" style with which the director has come to be identified.

Not only are there a lot of excerpts but also they tend to comprise entire scenes, often running to 4 or 5 minutes. Thus, we can better appreciate Ozu's dramaturgy along with his visual style. For example, Inoue has included the scene from *Brothers and Sisters of the Toda Family* (1941) when the prodigal son returns from China and berates his siblings for not treating their mother with appropriate respect. One by one they leave the formal dinner, with a reminder to pay the bill on their way out. While this scene strongly evokes the theme of filial loyalty that is repeated in *Tokyo Story*, another scene from *Early Summer* (1951) showcases the two actresses Setsuko Hara and Haruko Sugimura in a very different relationship than they play in the 1953 film (even if Hara once again plays the unmarried young woman). This is the pivotal scene in which Hara tells Sugimura (who plays an older woman) that she has decided to marry her son. After a long buildup to the announcement, for which the viewer is entirely unprepared, Sugimura explodes with the happiness that Hara seems to have such difficulty expressing.

Hara's enigmatic smile is in many ways the signature expression of Ozu's style, but there are many other actors, including most of the cast of *Tokyo Story*, who worked with him frequently. *I Lived, But . . .* includes fascinating interviews with many of the key actors of Japanese cinema, including Ineko Arima, Chikage Awashima, Nobu Nakamura, Shima Iwashita, Mariko Okada, Eijiro Tono, Haruko Sugimura and Yoko Tsukasa. Several dwell on the number of takes that Ozu required to capture a simple movement exactly the way he wanted. He often reduced the actor (most often an actress) to a trance-like state in which they were no longer aware of what they were doing. Despite the implicit cruelty of such a technique, Iwashita (speaking of *An Autumn Afternoon*) expresses gratitude toward Ozu for teaching her "how clearly these simple actions expressed deep sorrow." Sugimura describes how Ozu shot the scene in *Late Spring* in which she circles the room after Chishu Ryu and Setsuko Hara have left for the daughter's wedding. She didn't understand why Ozu demanded such precise repetition and rhythm until she saw the scene in the completed film.

These testimonials tend to paint Ozu as one of the most demanding directors who obtained exactly the performances he wanted with absolutely no allowance for personal inflection or expression. This tendency extended to his care over props and their placement, which were equally carefully chosen and positioned. He is quoted in the documentary as describing himself as a gardener, pruning trees and shrubs so that they won't move and grow however they want. His preoccupation with trimming excess speaks to his particular form of melodrama, which is, indeed, devoid of any excess.

Ozu remained single all his life, and a number of interviewees suggest that he was somewhat nervous around women in social situations, especially around his star actress Setsuko Hara. We also learn a bit about his drinking habits from Inoue's documentary. Ozu and his writing partner Kogo Noda routinely worked on their screenplays in Noda's villa in Kamakura where, according to Noda's widow, they averaged 100 bottles of sake per script. Interviews with several of Ozu's drinking buddies and their relatives are strongly reminiscent of scenes from some of the films. In the bar scene in *Tokyo Story*, for example, Chishu Ryu, deep in his cups, commiserates with his old friends about how "young people today have no backbone," before he stumbles home to fall asleep in a chair in his daughter's beauty parlor. The heavy drinking that characterized Ozu's life and films is symptomatic of his view of the world as at once bleak and light. It isn't black comedy so much as cheery resignation to the ways of the world. As one of the aphorisms in the *Tokyo Story* trailer puts it: "As long as life goes on, relationships between parents and children will bring boundless grief and endless joy."

Another platitude in the trailer states: "In the daily lives of ordinary people a sense of deep affection wells up." The simplicity of Ozu's films is his greatest deception. Director Yoji Yamada, who worked as an assistant to Ozu, says that it took him a long time to realize just how tall a mountain Ozu represented. From being chastised by the New Wave directors as the epitome of the "old guard" in the 1960s and 1970s, Ozu has come to be recognized as one of the key figures in the history of world cinema despite his conservatism.

The second documentary in the Criterion package is devoted to his international recognition. *Talking with Ozu* consists of commentaries by directors Stanley Kwan, Aki Kaurismäki, Claire Denis, Lindsay Anderson, Paul Schrader, Wim Wenders and Hou Hsiao-Hsien. Compiled in 1993, these are fairly predictable testimonials to the influence of Ozu on the work of these filmmakers. Each director has chosen a specific setting for their commentary, evoking Ozu's distinctive uses of urban and interior spaces. Perhaps the most original insight comes from the Taiwanese director Hou Hsiao-Hsien, for whom Ozu had the "detachment of a mathematician." Indeed, it is Ozu's objectivity that offsets the potential sentimentality of his narratives. While Ozu himself dismissed *Tokyo Story* as one of his most melodramatic films, the detachment implied in his formalist shooting style makes it melodrama of the highest order, as we have

**Fig. 14** *Tokyo Story* (Ozu, 1953).

come to understand melodrama more recently as a modernist mode.

Hou states the case most bluntly by noting that we are fortunate that Ozu lived in Japan when he did. Through the course of his 55 films, he found a way of articulating a sensibility that was not only very "Japanese" but also very "modern" in his perpetual ambivalence. In the context of a highly stylized *mise en scène*, and a rigorously defined world of social norms and customs, Ozu articulated the difficulty of being modern. It is difficult to be a modern man, and difficult to be a modern woman. The recurring themes of marriage and death link the rituals of family life to larger shifts in the social fabric. No explanation is given for the mother's death in *Tokyo Story* other than the stress of the overheated city that symbolically brings her down. And yet her death seems to clear a path for her daughter-in-law, Noriko, to be free of the burden of the past, even if it is a path taken reluctantly.

## *AN AUTUMN AFTERNOON*: FATHERS AND DAUGHTERS

Yasujiro Ozu's last film is known in English as *An Autumn Afternoon* (1962), although the Japanese title *Sanma no aji* translates as "The Taste of Mackerel." It was released in France in the 1970s as *Le gout du sake*, or "The Taste of Sake," which comes closest to indicating what the film is actually about, even if such literalness is antithetical to Ozu's poetics. This is a heavy-drinking film; the bulk of the action takes place in bars and restaurants. Reprising the themes of family and generational divides that became Ozu's staple postwar fodder, *An Autumn Afternoon* distils the family drama to a familiar pattern of formal rigor and emotional undercurrents. Stylistically, Ozu's signature techniques are refined to a stunning aesthetic system of time, space, line and color. As a final film, it retrospectively carries the weight of being at once emblematic and terminal.

Several plots are woven together in *An Autumn Afternoon*, and a constellation of characters are drawn into a social web, at the center of which is Hirayama, played by Chishu Ryu. Ozu's quintessential male actor, who played many fathers over the three decades of their collaboration, Ryu gives an extraordinary performance as a widower with three adult children. The key narrative line concerns Hirayama's relationship with his daughter Michiko (Shima Awashita), who is dangerously close to passing her best-before date as a marriage prospect. Michiko runs the household for her father and younger

**Fig. 15** *An Autumn Afternoon* (Ozu, 1962).

brother, but, although they all seem happy with this arrangement, social convention insists that Hirayama find a husband for his daughter. He tries hard to please her with a love match, but the man in question is already engaged, so in the end she marries a man who is described as healthy and dependable, and "a second son of a good family."

Ozu withholds from us anything further about Michiko's husband, who never appears as a character. As David Bordwell notes in his commentary, there is "no meeting of the fiancé, no courtship, no consultation with the parents." Not only is the very question of romance excluded, the wedding itself consists only of a single scene of Michiko dressed like a doll in her wedding dress, saying nothing and not looking very happy. Ozu skips the ceremony itself and cuts directly from Michiko's empty room to the home of Hirayama's friend Kawai (Nobuo Nakamura), where the two men drink whiskey along with their friend Horie. After some chat, Hirayama leaves them and drunkenly enters his favorite bar to see his favorite waitress and listen to his favorite military march before finally stumbling home to sit alone in the dark.

Michiko may never actually be seen weighing her limited options, but the film offers a number of different possible scenarios. For example, one of Hirayama's office assistants or OLs (office ladies) is 24 and getting married. Hirayama gives her an envelope of cash as a parting gift, as she will naturally be leaving her job. The worst fate for women is to be left alone to care for a widowed father. Haruko Sugimura plays such a daughter in the film, trapped in a dead-end life with a deadbeat father. Hirayama and Kawai describe her as being "cold and unfriendly," which is odd as she actually cries when they drag her drunken father home. Their friend Horie, meanwhile, has married a much younger woman who bosses him around.

Michiko's sister-in-law Akiko, played by Mariko Okada, is perhaps the most dynamic woman character in *An Autumn Afternoon*, but she is also depicted as a bossy new wife, whose husband — Michiko's brother Koichi — is seen wearing an apron in the kitchen. Koichi needs his wife's permission to buy the golf clubs he covets; and the two of them represent a new generation of Japanese consumers who are reinventing the rules of domestic life. Ozu thus depicts a range of possible domestic arrangements and roles for women, but the film is unambiguous in its nostalgic embrace of the old ways as a fading social ideal. Kawai's wife, for example, gracefully serves drinks to her guests along with a smattering of gossip.

In one of the film's final conversations, Hirayama complains that there is no point in having daughters or bringing them up. Clearly mourning his loss, his words nevertheless point to the misogynistic undertones of the film. As daughters, women just need to be married off. Hirayama's melancholy, however, underlines the profound contradictions implied in such social conventions. This is not to suggest that the film enacts a critique of those conventions, but it certainly dramatizes them, and it does so with great style, which is why I think it is ultimately within a framework of melodrama that this film needs to be understood.

*An Autumn Afternoon* is clearly not a film about women. It is a film about men and their roles in a changing world. One of the most notorious scenes of the film takes place in "Tory's bar" where "The Warship March" tune is always available on the jukebox. Hirayama meets one of his former wartime comrades and takes him out to Tory's, where his favorite waitress (Kyoka Kishida) works. Daisuke Kato, as the war buddy Sakamoto, marches, saluting to his former captain, down the length of the narrow bar. They imagine what the world would look like if Japan had won the war. "The blue-eyed ones would have chignon haircuts," suggests Sakamoto; but Hirayama demurs, saying that it was probably best that Japan lost. However, in the film's final scene, Hirayama hums a few bars of a military song in an expression of his loneliness after his daughter's marriage.

Within the framework of male friendship, Hirayama also has a number of models against which to compare himself. His friend Kawai, for example,

**Fig. 16** Chishu Ryu and Daisuke Kato in *An Autumn Afternoon* (Ozu, 1962).

appears to have fewer worries, perhaps due to his more conventional domestic arrangement. It is he who presides, with Hirayama, over the class reunion they organize for their former teacher. The class reunion is a recurring theme in Japanese cinema, often staging an encounter among old friends who assess one another's failures and successes. In this case the teacher becomes an object of sympathy and charity, as he is now a noodle-shop owner while his former students are all professionals. And yet "the Gourd's" main problem is simply that he has succumbed to the alcohol that flows so freely among these men. He serves as a warning to Hirayama, who seems destined to remain a widower. Despite his apparent success as a businessman, Hirayama is strangely disconnected from the world of his sons — and from the world of consumer products and baseball.

*An Autumn Afternoon* is one of Ozu's most rigorously stylized film, particularly with respect to his remarkable use of color. Red details punctuate almost every composition, standing out against a background palette of grays, browns and other muted tones. The Criterion package design emphasizes this aspect of the film with a choice of stills that highlights Ozu's aesthetics of color photography, and the DVD production is gorgeous. Because it is almost entirely studio-bound, the framing even of street scenes tends to be highly geometrical. As usual, transitional sequences punctuate the film, including a handful of exterior shots of buildings. But in this film there are no shots of laundry or teakettles. The world of Tokyo has been reduced to a bleak industrial system of corridors and closed rooms in which the splashes of red are the only real signs of life.

David Bordwell's commentary takes the viewer through the elaborate visual and narrative patterns that weave through the film. A complex play of themes and variations underscores a narrative that on its surface appears so aleatory following the rituals and routines of everyday life. Bordwell's narration actually goes further than the formalist thrust of his book on Ozu, filling in many of the details of the historical references and social context. Ozu's cinema has posed a long-standing conundrum for film scholars who are anxious to position him as a radical auteur, because he was in many respects extremely conservative, and, despite its formal achievements, this film stands in stark contrast to the emergent New Wave cinema of 1960s Japan.

The Criterion DVD also includes a valuable insight into a very different critical discourse on Ozu, in the form of excerpts from *Ciné-Regard*, a 1978 French television program. Critics Michel Ciment and Georges Perec enthusiastically discuss the belated "discovery" of Ozu in France, 20 years after the British and Americans. Their analysis is heavily influenced by the transcendentalist interpretation promoted by Paul Schrader in 1972 in which Ozu's style is related to Zen Buddhism, *haiku* poetry and *Noh* drama. Ciment claims that Ozu privileges the intensity of the lived moment "with no future and no past," a reading that seems particularly mismatched with a film that is as keenly historical as *An Autumn Afternoon*. However, Perec's observation that this is a "cinema in search of reality" seems more original and more helpful than either the formalist or the Orientialist interpretations of Ozu's modernity, and is particularly applicable to his final film.

The stylization of *An Autumn Afternoon* is, indeed, so rigorous that "reality" is restricted to the hints of emotional despair in Chishu Ryo's performance. Given the narrative impetus of the need to marry off one's daughter before it is "too late," the film creates a very strong sense of a society that runs like clockwork. Many of the scenes end abruptly, interrupted by characters suddenly coming and going after a glance at a clock or a watch. Twice in the film, Hirayama's friend Kawai plays tricks on him and in the process the viewer, too, is "set up." In the first instance, he says that their friend Horie has died from a dangerous combination of a weak heart and a young wife; and in the second that the marriage prospect he has found for Michiko is no longer available. Hirayama's gullibility is indicative of his lack of control over his own life, and the viewer is likewise at the mercy of Ozu's narrative gags.

The intersecting, overlapping conversations about money and marriage take place in a repetitive series of rigorously framed spaces, creating a sense of a mechanical everyday. Ozu's signature light waltz soundtrack that accompanies so many of the transitional sequences has a music-box quality that balances melancholy with an artificial upbeat sunniness. This is, indeed, a cinema that has eclipsed reality with design. The formal geometry of Ozu's framing and static camera turns the domestic and public spaces into an elaborate series of interlocking cubes. Only the decorative splashes of vivid red laced throughout the film point to the repressed desires and anxieties produced by this orderly world.

The Shochiku trailers for *An Autumn Afternoon* describe the film as a story about the "joys and sorrows of common people," and "a film about the love between a father and his children." It is promoted as a star-studded genre film, directed by a hard-working director. And yet, *An Autumn Afternoon* is in many ways exemplary of a "late cinema" made by an auteur who is himself slightly out of touch with his times. He is cynical toward the so-called "common people" who are either selfish consumers or poor alcoholics; and the story of love is in the end a story of loneliness. The stunning emptiness of Michiko's vacated room, dominated by an empty mirror, becomes emblematic of the film's central lacuna of the woman's desire and agency. *An Autumn Afternoon* may be set in 1962, but the sets and soundtrack tend to evoke a pervasive nostalgia that lifts Hirayama's loss onto a nationalist allegorical plane. He mourns his wife, he mourns his missing daughter, but most of all he mourns his youth in prewar and wartime Japan, a period that is dominated by a lost war of which it is impolite to speak.

## Chapter Three

# Kenji Mizoguchi and his Women

As an auteur, Mizoguchi is known mainly for two recurring features over his 24-year career: long, fluid camera movements and suffering women. He excelled in *jidai-geki*, although he worked in both *gendai-geki* and *jidai-geki* genres. His filmmaking technique, which relies heavily on complex tracking and crane shots, was championed by French film critics in the 1950s as an alternative to montage-based film practices. Critics have linked his elegant techniques to traditional Japanese idioms of painting and theater, and certainly his depiction of landscape and aristocratic architecture tends to bear this out. Darell Davis has convincingly argued that Mizoguchi developed a "monumental style" of cinema during the war years, in keeping with the imperialist mandate of reviving and rehabilitating traditional Japanese art forms. Certainly, his meticulous eye for period detail was instrumental in the reinvention of tradition that characterized the repressive regime of wartime Japan.

Despite his capitulation to the imperialist cause, Mizoguchi, like the vast majority of Japanese directors who had both prewar and postwar careers, switched very deftly to the democratic agenda of anti-feudalism after the war. Chief among his liberal-humanist topics was the liberation of women, which carried over from his prewar obsession with the plight of women trapped in impossible situations. Many of his films imply serious rebukes to institutions of power that keep women subjugated, and he is often referred to as a feminist director. However, his definition of *feminisuto*, or "special brand of Japanese

53

feminism" is an aesthetic appreciation of women, rather than a champion of women's rights. His women are beautiful in their self-sacrifice and their suffering, and his viewer may be moved to tears at the injustice of their plight, but neither social change nor transformation are ever presented as options. Social condemnation is balanced with pity and resignation. Sorrow is lined with guilt and self-abrogation, for it is a man's world in which Mizoguchi's women suffer.

## BEHIND THE SCENES OF *UGETSU MONOGATARI*

Criterion's release of Mizoguchi's 1953 masterpiece *Ugetsu monogatari* (*Tales of Moonlight and Rain*), together with a 1975 documentary on the director by Kaneto Shindo, provides a rather contradictory new perspective on this key film in Japanese film history. On the one hand, the film is revealed to be even more beautiful than was apparent from the poor 16 mm copies that many of us saw in film school. On the other, the many interviews with Mizoguchi's collaborators included in the Criterion package — which includes three separate interviews along with Shindo's documentary — make one seriously wonder how he managed to pull off such an achievement. The great director apparently never looked through the camera or contributed to the lighting design; he bullied the actors but never coached them; he rewrote the script on a daily basis; he delegated all the research and planning of the sets — insisting on changes only after everything was built — and he delegated all decisions about the magnificent score to the composer and his assistant directors. Nevertheless, within the culture of the Japanese studio system, Mizoguchi apparently wielded an authority based on a lengthy career of critically endorsed filmmaking that enabled him to achieve the results on display in *Ugetsu*.

Winning the Silver Lion in Venice in 1953, *Ugetsu* confirmed the status of Japanese cinema in world film culture, following the European success of Kurosawa's *Rashomon* (1950) in 1951. As Tony Raynes notes in his voice-over commentary, Mizoguchi may well have been motivated to compete with Kurosawa, who was much younger, with far fewer films to his credit than Mizoguchi. With *Ugetsu*, Mizoguchi made some significant alterations to his signature slow-paced, "scrolling" long takes, making a much more action-oriented, faster-paced film. Like *Rashomon*, *Ugetsu* is built from two short stories, from which a multi-character plot is developed. The parallel action and multi-plot construction may not pose the philosophical questions that *Rashomon* does, but *Ugetsu* demonstrates a similar narrative complexity in its smooth blending of reality and fantasy. Drawing on a variety of cinematic and performance techniques, *Ugetsu* follows *Rashomon* in its "modern" use of the medium in conjunction with a premodern story and setting.

The two original stories by Akinari Ueda on which *Ugetsu* is based have been newly translated and included in the Criterion package. Originally published in 1776 during the Edo period, the short tales are actually set in an earlier time, during the restless civil wars that preceded the stability of Ueda's own time. "The House in the Thicket" is about a man who leaves his wife for 7 years while he travels to the capital to make money by selling silk. When he returns, he is greeted by her ghost, who brings out his feelings of grief, guilt and longing. One of the highlights of *Ugetsu* is Mizoguchi's rendering of this return in one long take in which Genjuro (Masayuki Mori) enters his former home, finds it empty, circles round the back while the camera pans back inside, enters again, and finds his wife, Miyagi (Kinuyo Tanaka), seated by the hearth. It is a brilliant sleight of hand by which Mizoguchi and cameraman Kazuo Miyagawa produce the sense of the supernatural within the terms of a realist aesthetic.

The second Ueda story, "A Serpent's Lust," is about a man who is pursued and possessed by a seductive demon woman who poses as a princess. Mizoguchi and scriptwriter Yoshikata Yoda weave this into the first story by having Genjuro meet the mysterious Lady Wakasa (Machiko Kyo) during his 7-year absence from home. His romance with her, assisted by her faithful nurse Ukon (Kikue Mouri), is set among the beautiful architecture of a set modeled on the Katsura Imperial Villa. The Kutsuki Manor, as Wakasa's home is referred to in the film, is eventually revealed to have been merely a fantasy space into which Genjuro is summoned. Mizoguchi's compositions and Kyo's performance echo the style of the period, while the sets are adorned with the fabrics and objects of aristocratic life. Mizoguchi was notoriously exacting in his selection of props, and one of the pleasures of this new DVD is to be able to see the detail of the materials, not only in the Kutsuki Manor but also in the *kimono* and armor that also feature throughout the film. Once he learns he has been deceived, Genjuro eventually frees himself from the demon with the help of a priest. Nevertheless, the passion of his relationship with Lady Wakasa is palpable, and is probably the closest Mizoguchi ever came to depicting a sexual relationship in his entire career.

**Fig. 17** Machiko Kyo and Masayuki Mori in *Ugetsu Monogatari* (Mizoguchi, 1953).

The ethereal quality of the otherworldly romance in the Kutsuki Manor is contrasted with the brutal rape of Ohama (Mitsuko Mito), Genjuro's sister-in-law, who has accompanied the two men — Genjuro and his brother Tobei (Sakae Ozawa) — to the city. The only source for this subplot is a story by Guy de Maupassant about a man obsessed with achieving the honor of a military decoration. He finally manages to win the Legion of Honor, only by blinding himself to his wife's affair with a government official. In *Ugetsu*, Tobei displays an unquenchable ambition to become a samurai, and he finally succeeds by stealing the head of a beheaded general, only to find that his abandoned wife has become a prostitute. The story of Ohama, who is gang-raped by a group of rowdy soldiers before falling to prostitution, is added to the source material, and is emblematic of Mizoguchi's trademark narrative of the fallen woman. She and Tobei are finally reunited at the end of the film and she persuades him to denounce violence. Returning to the village after 7 years, he throws his armor into the river. The cunning wife of Maupassant's story is noticeably absent, perhaps because Mizoguchi's aesthetic sensibility can only accommodate the extremes of the femme fatale (Lady Wakasa) and the poor abandoned wives.

The way that *Ugetsu* is structured around two couples is suggestive of the influence of American cinema. Although Tobei may be Genjuro's brother, their relationship is not as clear or as vital as the two couples that are torn apart by the invasion of the village by warring factions of soldiers. It is rare in Japanese literature or film before the 1960s to find the couple as the primary social unit. More often, it is the larger family circle, including parents, grandparents, aunts and uncles. Genjuro and Miyagi have a son who is little more than a toy child, signaling that it is the nuclear family that is destroyed by the outbreak of war. The quest for upward mobility and its perennial failure is of course a mainstay of Hollywood cinema, soon to become a common theme of postwar Japanese cinema, but not commonly found in class-bound prewar Japanese film or literature. Miyagi is killed by starving fighters, roaming about like the stranded Japanese soldiers in the South Pacific, and indeed *Ugetsu* is often read as an antiwar film.

Scriptwriter Yoshikata Yoda confirms (in Shindo's documentary) that Mizoguchi did not intend *Ugetsu* to be an antiwar film, although the chaotic situation that surrounds the characters, linking their various storylines, is certainly evocative of the previous 15 years of Japanese history. From the beginning of the China war in 1937 (indeed, from the early 1930s) to the end of the Occupation, the nation endured a series of shifting ideologies, material scarcity, economic collapse, national defeat and foreign occupation. One could certainly interpret the departed soul of Miyagi as the loss of Japanese cultural integrity, lost through the greed for imperial power. By 1953, the nation was doomed to join the international community of industrial capitalism. The precious fantasy of cultural sovereignty was finally utterly ruined, like the bleak remains of the Kutuski Manor when Genjuro awakes from his dream.

Although such allegorical readings may have been far from Mizoguchi's mind, the aesthetic achievement of the film is very much in its depiction of instability. Kazuo Miyagawa, interviewed in 1992, notes that 70 percent of the film consists of crane shots. Indeed, the sense of chaos is felt in the constant movement of the camera: not only the sweeping overhead crane shots but also the shots that hover ever so slightly before the unfolding action. The constant shift of setting and the lack of conventional reverse-field cutting add to the pervasive sense of instability. In addition, the film boasts a truly remarkable soundtrack composed by Fumio Hayasaka. Based on musical ideas from traditional theater and performed mainly with drum, flute and monk chants, the score jettisons all conventions of "classical" film scoring for what Masahiro Shinoda describes as a truly avant-garde film score.

The interview with Shinoda (director of *Double Suicide* [1969], among other "New Wave" titles) was recorded in 2005, along with a separate interview with the first assistant director on *Ugetsu*, Tokuzo Tanaka. Like the interviews in Shindo's 2.5-hour documentary, these additional "special features" are mainly about the challenges of working with Mizoguchi, and are generally more gossipy than analytical. However, it is interesting that Shinoda and Tanaka offer two very different interpretations of the sexuality in *Ugetsu*. For Tanaka it is representative of "human greed," which is, indeed, one of the film's themes. Shinoda, however, reads the sexuality as a challenge to social conventions, effectively situating *Ugetsu* as an important precursor to his own more radical filmmaking of the 1960s and 1970s. Because sexuality was brought to (and enforced in) Japanese cinema during the Occupation, its status in 1953 is still very ambivalent, and as these contemporary views indicate, still open to very different readings.

Shindo, who also established himself as a director during the 1960s with *The Naked Island* (1960) and *Onibaba* (1964), won the top *Kinema Junpo* prize in 1975 for *Kenji Mizoguchi: The Life of a Film Director*. The documentary is a treasure trove of interviews with nearly 40 collaborators and friends of Mizoguchi, many of whom have subsequently passed away. Although at first it seems like a typical work of overblown hagiography, the portrait of the director that finally emerges is less than flattering. The anecdote that recurs most frequently, repeated by three different interviewees, is the story of the scar on Mizoguchi's back. Actress Urabe Kumeko was there when a prostitute named Yuriko Ichiro stabbed Mizoguchi after a lover's quarrel in the 1930s. Tokuzo Tanaka reports that Mizoguchi wore the scar like a badge of honor, boasting that "you can't make movies about women without this scar." Another assistant director, Seichiro Uchikawa, insists that this wound explains Mizoguchi's unique insight into the relationships between men and women.

As gossipy and anecdotal as is Shindo's documentary, it provides a privileged view of the culture of film production that made the Japanese studio system so successful. The social protocols and hierarchies, not to mention the codes of gendered behavior, enabled the system to function. Mizoguchi evidently relied on an assembly of actors and trusted technicians and craftsmen who were very accomplished at what they did, and worked extraordinarily hard to please the "Old Man." The film also provides a little history of the cinema of the 1920s, including interviews with director Daisuke Ito and writer Matsutaro Kawaguchi, and revisits the sites of many of the studios, locations and residences associated with Mizoguchi's long career. Shindo is particularly preoccupied with the Kyoto hospital where Mizoguchi died in 1956. Its emptiness and impenetrability come to stand in for the contradictions implicit in Mizoguchi's career.

Mizoguchi's womanizing was as notorious as his bullying of women on the set, and yet he thought of himself as someone who had a special insight into women's lives. Hisao Hoya says that Mizoguchi, emboldened by the spirit of democratic reform, told the prostitutes in a hospital he visited doing research for *Women of the Night* (1948), that he felt personally responsible for their plight. "It is men who are responsible for putting you here," he announced to the women, who were anxious for an autograph from the great director. On the other hand, many of the actresses relate in detail how Mizoguchi pushed them to the edge in order to get them to perform as he wanted. Shindo is relentless in his interviews, and the back of his head appears in almost every frame of the film, although his face is barely glimpsed. It's an unusual technique, but it creates a sense of continuity and intimacy that finally pays off in his interview with Kinuyo Tanaka, the star of ten of Mizoguchi's postwar films. Many of the interviewees suggest without hesitation that Mizoguchi was in love with Tanaka. Despite his two wives and many mistresses, Tanaka is repeatedly said to be the real love of his life.

When Shindo confronts the actress with these rumors, she says she welcomes the opportunity to dispel them. She argues that Mizoguchi was not in love with her, but with the women she played in his films, women like Miyagi in *Ugetsu*, who are beautiful in their suffering. He was in love with a certain image of women, and besides, she says, he lacked humor and was too preoccupied with his art. He was a difficult man, and she could not see him as a good husband. Indeed, Koga Kogawa claims that most of Mizoguchi's women had bad lives and were from poor backgrounds, women who perhaps didn't know better — didn't know to avoid him. In touristy snapshots from Venice, where Tanaka and Mizoguchi went in 1953 with *Ugetsu*, the two of them appear awkward together, more like acquaintances than friends. Tokuzo Tanaka says that, while Mizoguchi demanded many retakes from most of his actors, he usually let Kinuyo Tanaka get away with her first take, saying it was perfect every time. Clearly, there was some kind of chemistry at work, but one that mixed shyness and distance in larger parts than the complicity and mutual understanding that the term usually implies.

The interviews contained in this DVD package shed a great deal of light on the production of *Ugetsu*, and while they might break the spell of this mesmer-izing film for some viewers, they also suggest how Mizoguchi's "special effects"

**Fig. 18** Kinuyo Tanaka in *Ugetsu Monogatari* (Mizoguchi, 1953).

were created from sheer human endurance and perseverance. The ghostly scene of the two families crossing Lake Biwa through shrouds of mist was shot in a studio-built pool in which assistant directors stood in freezing water pushing the boats through clouds of smoke that refused to waft as planned. Likewise, two anecdotes fill in the details of Mori's performance in the film's final scene of Genjuro's homecoming. Given minimal direction from Mizoguchi, Mori finally went to cameraman Miyagawa for help with the scene. In a very giggly interview, Miyagawa claims that he simply told Mori that he had a chest of drawers inside him, so he should start with the top drawer, which is precisely what the actor did. Kinuyo Tanaka reports that everyone, including herself, was extremely nervous about shooting this scene, in which the level of tension on the set was much higher than usual. In a daze, following the shooting of the famous scene, she saw Mizoguchi lighting Mori's cigarette, an act she had never seen the director perform for anyone. Indeed, for all the attention that Machiko Kyo and Kinuyo Tanaka have received for *Ugetsu*, Mori's central role is often overlooked. It is arguably the tightly wound energy of this actor (who died in 1973) that provides the film's central, sustaining momentum.

With all the materials added to this new release of *Ugetsu*, we can finally recognize its achievement within the context of modern Japan. As the trailer makes abundantly clear, with its overblown orchestral score, its "fierce and awe-inspiring" tone, and its exaggeration of the film's melodramatic and action elements — its sex and violence — *Ugetsu* is the product of a commercial industry. Mizoguchi's fidelity to period detail could only have been accomplished

**Fig. 19** Masayuki Mori in *Ugetsu Monogatari* (Mizoguchi, 1953).

with the vast resources at his disposal at Daiei studio in Kyoto. He was bound
for Venice, and determined to impress the world with his achievement, stopping
at nothing to prove himself among the world's top directors. If his film tended
to confirm an Orientalist conception of modern Japanese art, it was also open
to a wealth of interpretation that is far from exhausted 53 years later.

## *SANSHO THE BAILIFF*: ELEVENTH-CENTURY FAMILY MELODRAMA

*Sansho the Bailiff* (1954) is the third of a trio of Mizoguchi films that won major
awards in Venice in the 1950s. Like *Ugetsu monogatari* and *The Life of Oharu*
(1952), *Sansho* is a period film featuring Kinuyo Tanaka as a long-suffering
woman living in violent and oppressive times. This trilogy effectively made
Mizoguchi the darling of European cinephiles in the 1950s, enamored as they
were of his long-take shooting style, passionate performances and Orientalist
aesthetics. The film draws on a range of sources for its distinctive, stylized
look, including *Noh* drama and *kabuki* theater, Japanese woodblock prints and
Buddhist iconography and thematics. The story itself is based on a folk tale said
to be part of an ancient oral tradition, but which was written up and published
in 1915 by the novelist Ogai Mori.

This is indeed a beautiful film and it no doubt inspired and excited European
audiences to the potential of cinema to create the atmosphere of another world.
The setting in a distant past and a distant land is at once fantastic and realist.

With its depiction of poverty, thematics of oppression and self-sacrifice, it plays all the right notes of postwar humanism. And yet, the film might be just a bit too perfect, a bit too familiar and a bit too overwrought for everyone's taste. Seen in the light of post-postwar post-humanism, it might be seen as a remarkable confluence of Buddhist aesthetics and bourgeois values, testimony to the ability of cinema to bring together the "impermanence and futility" of Zen with the dramatic excess of high melodrama.

According to Mizoguchi's assistant director Tokura Tanaka, Mizoguchi was more interested in the theme of the slavery system than the family melodrama that ends up dominating the storyline. To be sure, the slavery system of the eleventh century is depicted in some detail, mainly through the eyes of the brother and sister, Zuchio (Yoshiaki Hanayagi) and Anju (Kyoko Kagawa), who are captured as children and grow up within the confines of the camp. Their slave-master Sansho (Eitaro Shindo) is demonically villainous, branding those who disobey him on the forehead with his mark. The excessive brutality of these scenes is expressed mainly in the terrified faces and screams of Sansho's victims and their witnesses. Zuchio internalizes the master's evil when he steps up himself to do the branding. It is against the horrors of such outrageous violence that the film's notoriously beautiful landscape compositions gain their aesthetic weight.

With its extremes of good and evil, darkness and light, *Sansho the Bailiff* is film melodrama at its finest. The themes of sacrifice, suffering and loss do not, however, have any ironic edge. This is a film that takes itself very seriously, and if there is any allegorical relation to postwar Japan, its outlook is thoroughly infused with loss. Zuchio eventually escapes the slave compound, and is redeemed from his terrible act of branding through the sacrificial act of his sister. Bearing a treasured Buddhist amulet given to him by his father, he is finally recognized by "the authorities" as a noble man. Given a title, he decrees the end of slavery. Christlike, he returns to Sansho's camp and proclaims the freedom of his former consignees, fomenting a slave rebellion as Sansho attempts to quash the orders. However, Zuchio does not have the authority to issue such a decree of liberation, so he in turn is cast out of office and the critique of institutional authority is upheld. He renounces his post in order to search for his long-lost mother.

Tamaki, the mother played by Kinuyo Tanaka, has fallen on hard times herself. Imprisoned in an island brothel, she is rendered lame and blind by her captives. The final reconciliation between mother and son, burdened by the loss of father and daughter, is just about as weepy as it gets. The desolate setting of a run-down beach hut accentuates the sense of devastation while the soundtrack, combining orchestral strings with atonal Japanese flute, rises to a fever pitch. The discordance of Fumio Hayasaka's soundtrack is really what saves *Sansho* from falling into maudlin and sentimental family drama. Several other key scenes, such as the children being cruelly separated from their mother and nurse by wretched slave traders, are pierced by the flute rising in pitch and volume. This soundtrack, together with Kazuo Miyagawa's cinematography and

**Fig. 20** Yoshiaki Hanayagi and Kinuyo Tanaka in *Sansho the Bailiff* (Mizoguchi, 1954).

lighting design, distinguishes the film as the classic work it is credited to be.

The centerpiece of *Sansho*, the scene that is perhaps most emblematic of the film's aesthetic, is the one in which Anju escapes Sansho's camp, only to wade slowly into the water and disappear under a ripple of concentric waves. The old woman entrusted to guard her, who has in fact released her, witnesses the act, which is shot through a foreground frame of foliage. The scene is rich in pathos and it works cinematically as a surprising narrative twist: losing a central character like this, through suicide, is unusual in narrative cinema. Despite the Buddhist iconography, Anju's great sacrifice that allows her brother to escape bearing a sick fellow slave on his back to a nearby temple is, nevertheless, hard to swallow. The two children until that point were equals, abandoned equally by their father, stolen from their mother and enslaved by Sansho. While Zuchio was corrupted by the slave-master's brutality, Anju heard the mournful sound of her mother's voice, transposed through a song overheard by another woman.

Especially when Zuchio is given the special hat of high office, it is evident that this is a film about patriarchy and it discontents. Anju's sacrifice is the key to social stability and moral order.

The Criterion release of *Sansho the Bailiff* includes Ogai Mori's rendition of the original tale from 1915, and also another version, translated from anthropological sources of the legend. While Mizoguchi's screenplay was adapted from Mori's version, the older one tells quite a different story. Entitled "An Account of the Life of the Deity of Mount Iwaki," the traditional story is told in the first person by Anju herself, who becomes a goddess by virtue of her suffering. She becomes a great deity with powers over an entire province, with healing powers and the ability to fly. She mentions her brother only as an afterthought at the end of the story. In the modern version, however, the gender codes of maternity and authority have replaced the ancient powers attributed to the feminine. The modern version is in many ways a classic tale of an emasculated father whose son eventually replaces him along with the symbolic order he represents. The story has, furthermore, all the classic features of nineteenth-century melodrama, including blindness and the recognition of virtue. The token Buddha fetish is in itself a phallic symbol of power, virtue and truth.

Such a crude Oedipal analogy may be offensive to those viewers who privilege the spiritual and traditional elements of the story, but I think it is important to recognize just how modern the tale really is, and how the two narrative traditions, drawn from ancient and modern sources, are so thoroughly intertwined. Ogai Mori's narrative was written shortly after the critical suicide of General Nogi and his wife in 1912, marking a significant loss of faith in the empire and its paternalistic structure of authority. In Mori's version of the story, the absent father has been exiled because the governor of his province had been convicted of a crime. His exile is proof of loyalty and upholds the principle of authority underpinning Confucian ideology; the son frees the slaves, but does not relinquish his own newfound rank. In Mizoguchi's version, both father and son are anti-feudalist liberal humanists who disobey the chain of command to uphold moral principles. Mori's version of the fairy tale adapts it to his "modern" purposes of proto-militarization and empire-building, while Mizoguchi reworks it again for his postwar anti-feudalist agenda.[1] The father in the film is absolved after his death, but Zuchio finds his redemption not in his moral conviction but in the pathos of his grieving mother. For Mizoguchi, it is the critique that is in itself a purifying gesture; moral authority does not lie in the military hierarchy but in the "moral occult" of the suffering woman.

The *jidai-geki* genre is often characterized by complex political negotiations between men, and this film is no exception. When Zuchio is recognized for who he is, a series of men with extraordinary hats manage his promotion. The costumes are somewhat unusual, as few Japanese films are set in this remote eleventh-century period. Mizoguchi's crew based their designs on careful research, designing flowing gowns and puffy hats for the men and diaphanous gowns for the women, with Heian-period hairstyles and eyebrows and enormous lacquered hats. Kinuyo Tanaka is seen repeatedly windblown, her long hair whipping up in the sea breeze as she calls relentlessly for her lost children. In true melodramatic fashion, history is denoted by style. The costume design, no less than the stylized compositions of characters in huge architectural sets — ministerial villas and temples — and natural settings framed by water and

**Fig. 21** Yoshiaki Hanayagi in *Sansho the Bailiff* (Mizoguchi, 1954).

trees, give the film its majestic and spiritual feel.

Miyagawa's cinematography renders the extremes of good and evil through sharp contrasts and subtle lighting. Most of the film was shot in studio, but even outside the studio Miyagawa and Mizoguchi painstakingly created fields of silver grass, decorously drooping branches, and strategically placed trees. Flowing water in this film always sparkles and glows. Nature is, indeed, larger than life, taking on the kind of mystical powers attributed to it in Buddhist and Shinto tales. As a social politics, however, the themes of suffering, sacrifice and resignation are at odds with antislavery activism.

Perhaps the best way of appreciating *Sansho* is as a silent film, and not only because of its great use of expressive cinematography and evocative soundtrack. The storytelling method consists of cryptic fragments of visual information offered with minimal dialogue, like the oversimplified condensation of silent film narrative. This shorthand style is, moreover, linked to the Manichean depiction of social oppression, with tyrants and their victims clearly distinguished. Zuchio's father, for example, is demoted and exiled at the beginning of the film for attempting to spare his famine-struck people (farmers and peasants presumably) from raising money for war. The general apparently doesn't care if they are starving and suggests that they all be killed instead. The society of the time is depicted as heartless and somewhat absurd. Tamaki and her children, traveling alone to rejoin their exiled father, are refused shelter by local families because of rampant slave traders in the area. The governing authorities seem to have sided with the outlaws rather than the good citizens; indeed, as the opening titles inform us, in this era "mankind had not yet awakened as human beings." But when Zuchio finally frees the slaves and regains the power lost to his father, he abruptly renounces it all, returning to the humble outfit of a common man, presumably leaving the freed slaves to fend for themselves.

The Criterion package for this film includes interviews with assistant director Tokura Tanaka, actress Kyoko Kagawa, and film critic Tadao Sato. Kagawa describes Mizoguchi's process of directing actors in some detail, claiming she learned a great deal from him, despite his demanding practice of multiple rehearsals and tests for every shot. She notes that it did not feel like a collaboration so much as an ongoing attempt to please the director. Both she and Sato comment on the ways that Mizoguchi required actors to react to one another in his long-take shooting style. Because he largely eschewed shot-reverse-shot sequences, the actors were required to work together and "react" to one another, in terms of both blocking and dialogue.

For his part, critic Tadao Sato repeats the familiar adage that Mizoguchi's preoccupation with suffering women was bound up with his own guilt about the women he had caused to suffer. Sato suggests that all Japanese (men, presumably) should feel equally sorry for the wrongs dealt out against women over the past centuries. In keeping with this *feminisuto* sensibility, neither Kinuyo Tanaka's performance nor Kagawa's really endow their characters with personality; rather, they embody icons of grief. As Zuchio, Yoshiaki Hanayagi performs with far more energy and dynamism, perhaps due to his theater training, or because his character is substantially more active. The film does feature a surprising number of close-ups for a Mizoguchi film, but the characters are better defined through costume and makeup than through facial expression or dialogue.

The classic status of *Sansho* in Japanese film history may help in the end to pinpoint some of the deeply rooted ideological contradictions in postwar Japan. On one hand, the film's message — that man must be merciful to be human — passed on from father to son, is very much in keeping with postwar humanism and the renunciation of violence. On the other, the deification of nature and aesthetics of resignation, passivity and asceticism that are embedded in a Buddhist sensibility do not sit well with the activism of emancipation. In the Japanese period film there is no middle class, and Mizoguchi cannot in the end transcend the feudal class structure that produced the slave system that is demonized in the film. The pervasive grief and mourning is not for anything other than an ancient culture reconceived as a collapsed patriarchy. In this light, the climactic reunion of mother and son signals a familiar resolution of the family drama and the future of a modern bourgeoisie.

*Chapter Four*

# Men with Swords and Men with Suits: The Cinema of Akira Kurosawa

ifty-one years after the sensational screening of *Rashomon* (1950) in
Venice, Akira Kurosawa was the first Japanese director whose films were
widely released in digital form. In Japan as well, Kurosawa's was the first
large oeuvre to be made available on DVD. In 1951 *Rashomon* introduced
Japanese cinema to international audiences, which greatly enhanced Kurosawa's
profile at home. Has nothing changed in 50 years? Or has so much changed that
Kurosawa has come to stand in for a national cinema that is in desperate need
of cultural capital? A new documentary, *Kurosawa* (2001) by Adam Low, goes
some distance in explaining the status of Japan's first truly international director,
although it tends to buy into the usual biographical mythology of Kurosawa's
samurai heritage and covert identification with all his main characters, especially those played by Toshiro Mifune.

Another documentary, entitled *A Message from Akira Kurosawa: For Beautiful
Movies*, produced in 2000 by Kurosawa's son Hisao, is an even more uncompro-
mising work of hagiography, and includes extensive interview footage with the
great man himself. The director is depicted as an artist who single-handedly
revolutionized world cinema through his invention of countless techniques
and his dedication to the beauty of cinema. Bowing to the camera, Kurosawa's

daughter Kazuko graciously thanks all the viewers who have come to appreciate her father's films. Both documentaries illustrate the director's involvement in the many aspects of the production process, from scriptwriting and costume design to editing and music composition, but, in each case, he is seen to be greatly removed from any historical or industrial context. Aside from the crises of the Great Kanto Earthquake of 1923 and the Pacific War, which ostensibly acquainted him with death and suffering, Kurosawa is depicted as a creative genius operating outside social and cultural pressures. And yet the director himself has admitted that making a film is like a battle in which the director is the commander on the front line, suggesting that creative genius may not in itself be sufficient for great filmmaking.

Kurosawa can, however, be positioned within an industrial mode of production and specific historical conditions. Stuart Galbraith IV's dual biography of Kurosawa and Mifune, *The Emperor and the Wolf* (2001), despite its title, serves as one of the best industrial histories of Japanese cinema available in English. Galbraith does an excellent job of situating Kurosawa within the production practices of the Japanese studio and star systems, the international film marketplace, critical discourse in Japan and the United States, and the struggle for financing that plagued the director from the early 1960s to his death in 1998. The book also contains complete filmographies for both actor and director, and a comprehensive index that will make it a valuable reference work.

Teruyo Nogami, Kurosawa's long-time script supervisor, has published an English translation of her memoir, providing elaborate detail about the social and institutional conditions in which Kurosawa worked. As the only woman besides the actresses on Kurosawa's sets, Nogami's perspective is a rare insight into the male-dominated world of the Japanese film industry. An unabashed fan of the man she worked for from 1951 until his death in 1998, Nogami reveals few details of her own life and feelings outside of Kurosawa's shooting schedule. According to Donald Richie, she was the only person with whom the director did not lose his temper.[1] Her descriptions of the social activities and decision-making processes around Kurosawa's productions constitute a veritable ethnography of the studio system in action. Although she offers plenty of evidence of Kurosawa's fearsome temper, she also describes how he presided over nightly dinners, entertaining his cast and crew with stories and song.

Nogami also appears in the Toho Masterworks series "It's Wonderful to Create," from which Criterion has excerpted episodes on many of their Kurosawa releases. These TV spots feature interviews with many of Kurosawa's cast and crew members, including production designer Yoshiro Muraki, composer Masaru Sato and property master Koichi Hamamura, among others. Steeped in trivia and anecdotes, each episode is devoted to a different film in Kurosawa's oeuvre, and they are fascinating insights into the director's production methods and techniques. Not lacking in respect for the master, the series also demonstrates and exemplifies the hierarchies and pecking orders characteristic of Japanese institutions. It is also very evident from these episodes that, despite the studio context, Kurosawa and his crews were constantly improvising, innovating and collaborating to solve creative problems and find new means of expression. As writer, editor and director of all his films, Kurosawa operated as an independent director within a studio system that encouraged loyalty and hard work. Time and again, we hear "Kurosawa really praised me when I did such and such," accounts of how various shots were achieved, and memories loaded with fascinating trivia and anecdotes about the productions. These Toho featurettes, while produced by the studio, and evidently promotional and hagiographic, nevertheless go a long way in demonstrating how Kurosawa managed to work successfully within a commercial film industry while producing examples of film art.

The Criterion collection includes quite a number of wonderfully remastered titles, and many are packaged with a full array of commentaries, trailers, booklets and special features. Many of these extras, such as the Toho Masterworks series, also help us to better understand Kurosawa's methods and practice. The Criterion edition of *Seven Samurai* (1954) includes a fascinating 2-hour interview shot in 1993 and produced by the Directors Guild of Japan in which Nagisa Oshima grills Kurosawa about the director system and his early years at PCL and Toho. Kurosawa describes it as a system based on military cadet training. Assistant directors were required to learn every component of a production, from costume design to location scouting, editing and sound recording. He complains that, despite this excellent training, once assistants are promoted to directors, they tend to remain submissive to their studio and do little to retain their rights to their own work. Oshima and Kurosawa concur in a mutual critique of censorship, despite the fact that Kurosawa's wartime experience was a radically different encounter with censors than Oshima's 1970s challenge of obscenity legislation. In any case, Oshima does not challenge his interviewee on any points, but does dig a bit deeper into questions of institutional practice and social themes than one finds in the Toho-produced documentaries.

In fact Kurosawa's career was very much tied to the vicissitudes of Japanese history and to the ups and downs of the film industry. Donald Richie describes Kurosawa as a specialist in the *shokai-mono* — films with "social themes" — into which category he includes both *jidai-geki* and *gendai-geki*. Born in 1910, Kurosawa's apprenticeship and directorial debut was at the height of the Pacific War. Although he admits that he did nothing to resist Japan's militarism, only two of his films can be described as propaganda: a factory film called *The Most Beautiful* (1944) and *Sanshiro Sugata Part Two* (1945). The release of *The Men Who Tread on the Tiger's Tail* (1945) was delayed by both the Japanese and Occupation censors, as neither government was pleased with the film's playful treatment of a traditional text (too subversive for the former; too "feudal" for the latter).[2] With *No Regrets for Our Youth* (1946), Kurosawa spearheaded the pro-democracy objectives of the Occupation regime, although the script went through so many review committees, it ends up being somewhat confused, both ideologically and aesthetically. Galbraith's discussion of the productions of the 1940s reveals the harsh conditions in which these films were made. Many of his interviewees recall how hungry they were during the shoots, and how the scarcity of personnel and materials affected many production decisions. For example, there are no women at all in *Tiger's Tail*, according to Galbraith, because all the women and children had been evacuated out of the city.[3] Low's documentary includes some stunning archival footage of a devastated Tokyo, and some excellent newsreel footage of the Hirohito surrender that so affected the nation's self-image.

## KUROSAWA AND JAPAN

The implicit tension between "Kurosawa" and "Japan" is captured by a recurring motif in Adam Low's documentary: the display of Kurosawa's films on high-tech electronic screens and video devices. Mifune's spectacular death scene in *Throne of Blood* (1957), in which he is assaulted by a barrage of arrows on a castle balcony, is projected on a digital screen on a building in downtown Tokyo, nestled within the loud neon signs and busy architecture of the city. Interviews with Machiko Kyo and Clint Eastwood are accompanied by electronic view-ing devices placed carefully in Kyo's Japanese room, and in Eastwood's ranch landscape. James Coburn watches a scene from *Seven Samurai* on a particularly beautifully designed home-viewing gadget. The juxtaposition of these digital devices and Kurosawa's *jidai-geki* reinforces the classicism of his cinema. His films have become emblematic of the Japanese past, which seems far removed from the technological present.

Indeed, this is perhaps the dominant perception of Kurosawa, the master of the samurai genre, a last link to a vanishing history. And yet, such an image of Kurosawa does not do justice to his status as a modernist, as an innovator whose contribution to world cinema lies in his ability to work in the techno-logical languages of image and sound recording — to develop a visual culture of Japanese modernity. Kurosawa's career is in many ways emblematic of the profound misunderstandings between Western and Japanese cultures. While Westerners are often said to understand and appreciate his films better than Japanese, they tend to think of them as representative of a national culture. In fact, over the course of his career, although he has gained great notoriety in Japan, he has never been typical of mainstream Japanese cinema.

It may be true that by the late stages of his career Kurosawa had become out of synch with the times, but in the 1950s, films such as *Rashomon, Ikiru* (1952) and *Seven Samurai* effectively put Japanese cinema on the map. *Yojimbo* (1961) and *High and Low* (1963) were also extremely contemporary works. The cyni-cism of the former and the snazzy architecture of the latter were very much in keeping with the art cinema of the period, and he did it all with style. Galbraith quotes *LA Weekly*'s Tom Carson on Kurosawa in 1990: "If anything, in the 1950s and early '60s, he was the director who reinvented art house movie going as pure visceral sensation." For Galbraith, Carson is "hopelessly out of touch," but I think there may be something to this recognition of Kurosawa as a director for whom visual style is paramount. Certainly his late career comeback was due to support from those bastions of action and spectacle Francis Ford Coppola and Steven Spielberg, who produced *Kagemusha* in 1980.

Critical debate about Kurosawa tends to be plagued by questions about his Japaneseness and his alleged pandering to Western tastes. In fact, what makes his cinema so interesting is his ability to draw from a global cultural heritage that incorporates Japanese traditions as well as Western literature and

Hollywood cinema. Kurosawa himself claimed to be committed to Japanese audiences and was disappointed that foreigners tended to appreciate his work more than Japanese, who he claimed were sadly out of touch with their own cultural history. However, Kurosawa's popularity outside Japan is hardly due to the accuracy with which he represents Japanese history but more often, a combination of Orientalism and cinephilia.

The question of Kurosawa's "Japaneseness" is placed most centrally in Mitsuhiro Yoshimoto's book on Kurosawa, although discussion of the films tends to get bogged down in Yoshimoto's larger metacritical project of interrogating the methods of Japanese film studies. Nevertheless, his point that Kurosawa "arouses the feeling of anxiety in Japanese and Western critics because his films problematize Japan's self-image and the West's image of Japan," is well taken.[4] Yoshimoto explains how Kurosawa engages in Japanese theater history and dramatic genres, refiguring the wealth of traditional Japanese culture within the cinema. As the juxtaposition of the *jidai-geki* with the high-tech, high-rise neon skyline of Tokyo suggests, "Japaneseness" is not a static concept and it is an aspect of global modern culture. Kurosawa may be deeply indebted to Shakespeare, Dostoevsky and John Ford, but we also need to remember how he in turn influenced the genre of the western in the 1960s.

**Fig. 22** Toshiro Mifune, Diasuke Kato and Tatsuya Nakadai in *Yojimbo* (Kurosawa, 1961).

*Yojimbo*, for example, not only provided the blueprint for the plot of *A Fistful of Dollars* (1964) but also Ennio Morricone's famous score was prefigured by Masaru Sato's incredible use of jazz and swing motifs in a period film. *Yojimbo* is an extraordinary modernist work, even if it is set in 1860. The ironic anachronistic score only works, of course, in conjunction with Mifune's swaggering performance. As the ronin casually sells himself to the highest bidder and laughs as the miserable town destroys itself, this is genre revision of the highest order. The selfish cynicism of the wandering warrior is a fabulous challenge to the glorified code of *bushido*, the samuri code of loyalty to a lord. Even if Leone and Eastwood managed to find an equally sardonic style for their cycle of films, they were never able to match the ironic playfulness of the original.

Comparing Kurosawa's samurai films with the American westerns they inspired, such as the Leone films and *The Magnificent Seven* (1960), it is evident that these films were not made for the small screen. One of the first things one notices about the DVD releases of Kurosawa's films is the prevalence of long shots and the infrequency of close-ups. One of the most remarkable motifs in the *jidai-geki* such as *Throne of Blood*, *Kagemusha* (1980) and *Ran* (1985), are the ranks of soldiers bearing fluttering banners on their backs. They move like rippling waves of men across landscapes and through elaborate castle architecture. *Sanjuro* (1962) likewise features a gaggle of nine samurai who behave like a single nine-headed character. The seven samurai of the film thus named are framed and reframed in compositions that visually structure their various relationships. While much ink has been spilled over Kurosawa's construction of the hero and the self in a culture where individualism is traditionally sublimated to the good of the group, we also need to recognize that groups of men are very much at the center of many of the films.

Another excellent supplemental feature on the Criterion release of *Seven Samurai* on the film's origins and influences includes interviews with leading Kurosawa scholars Stephen Prince, David Desser, Joan Mellen, Tony Rayns, Donald Richie and Tadao Sato. These critics explain how Kurosawa reinvented a genre that before the war was not referred to as a "samurai" genre but "sword

**Fig. 23** *Kagemusha* (Kurosawa, 1980).

films" or *chambara*. Even then, the samurai hero often tended to be at odds with social codes, hierarchies and institutions. Kurosawa further "humanized" and individualized the sword-fighting heroes, while ramping up the depiction of violence, historical realism and character psychology. The documentary includes rare footage of prewar samurai films, along with illustrations from the visual arts and theater predating cinema. The production of *Seven Samurai* drew on substantial research into the sixteenth-century period, while revising the genre conventions of a popular form. Its epic scope at 207 minutes made it a "classic" for both Japanese and Western audiences. In place of *bushido*, Kurosawa infused the genre with class analysis, romance and humanitarian altruism. In many respects *Seven Samurai* was the first samurai film, even while its international success made it the first popular Asian film internationally. Its period setting may have blinded audiences to its contemporaneity and modernity, but its innovations should not in turn blind us to its John Ford and American western–influenced conventions of gender and male bonding.

**Fig. 24** Takashi Shimura and Isao Kimura in *Seven Samurai* (Kurosawa, 1954).

## KUROSAWA'S MEN

Kurosawa's final film, *Madadayo* (1993), about a retired professor and his gang of *sensei*-worshiping male students, is in many ways the epitome of the theme of homosociality. The men in *Madadayo* age very little in the 20 years (1943 to 1962) that the film covers but, like many of Kurosawa's male characters, they are consistently dressed in suits and ties. In fact half of Kurosawa's 31 features are set in the twentieth century. Men with swords appear in only nine of his films; these are the titles that have achieved the most notoriety, in Japan and internationally. Toshiro Mifune is closely associated with the samurai genre but he also performed in many of Kurosawa's *gendai-geki*, including *High and Low*, *Stray Dog* (1949), *Drunken Angel* (1948) and *The Bad Sleep Well* (1960). All of these films are set in an urban milieu and are set on a much smaller scale that makes them much more appropriate for home video than the samurai epics. The preoccupation with the *jidai-geki* is as true of the Asian perception of the director as it is of the so-called Western perspective. Kurosawa's Japaneseness consists in his ability to bring the Japanese past to life, which is to say, to bring it into the realm of modern culture, while his equally important engagement with his own historical epoch remains relatively neglected.

**Fig. 25** Tatsuo Matsumura in *Madadayo* (Kurosawa, 1993).

From 1948 to 1965 — arguably the peak years of the director's career — the groups of men with swords and suits are always subservient to the heroic figure of Mifune. The relationship between the actor and the director is one of the most crucial pairings of film history, as their collaboration is ultimately responsible for the success of Kurosawa's best films. Mifune entered the acting profession reluctantly. In 1946, desperate for work after being discharged from the army (he never saw action), he applied for a job as a cameraman at Toho, but ended up in the New Face contest, where Kurosawa saw his audition and recommended that he be hired. In 1948, in his first film with Kurosawa — *Drunken Angel* — Mifune plays a gangster with tuberculosis and a Bogart-inspired slouch that had never been seen before in Japanese film. In *Stray Dog* he plays a cop who tries to retrieve his pistol from a gang of pickpockets and black-marketeers.

In these two films, he develops the persona of the tough but despondent post-war Japanese man, who is overwhelmed by the urban destruction and moral decay of the era, but nevertheless exudes a certain flair among the ashes.

**Fig. 26**  Toshiro Mifune in *Drunken Angel* (Kurosawa, 1948).

Mifune was above all a physical actor, who relied mainly on his athletic ability to move his bulky body quickly and gracefully. His bandit character in *Rashomon* and his samurai-wannabe in *Seven Samurai* are both somewhat comic roles. He spends much of both movies in a low crouch, leaping about with buttocks bared. The samurai of *Yojimbo*, *Sanjuro* and *The Hidden Fortress* (1958) are men who are "hard to kill," but Mifune also took on more introspective characters. For example, his businessmen figures in *The Bad Sleep Well* and *High and Low* are complex portrayals of modern Japanese men, even if he still relies principally on his gruff voice and bulky size. These are men surrounded by corruption and greed who, nevertheless, retain the necessary moral integrity to keep home and hearth from total destruction.

At the age of 24 Mifune played a 70-year-old man in *I Live in Fear* (a.k.a. *Record of a Living Being*, 1955), a performance that is greatly aided by makeup, thick glasses and a hunched back. While his characterization of a man who insists on moving his entire extended family to Brazil to be safe from atomic destruction is convincing, the film itself is not. Like *Scandal* (1950), which is about tabloid journalism, *I Live in Fear* is an attempt on Kurosawa's part to respond to contemporary events; both films are interesting more for their

ocial anthropology with its focus on kinship rela-
the beginning anthropology developed a distinc-
ation and detailed recording in 'field notes', known
much on 'primitive' or 'tribal' societies – people
at were thought to be significant ways, although in
d concepts have been applied to Western societies.
ts for many years were backward in applying their
and childhood. Anthropologists tended to rely on
ehaviour and adult beliefs, to be interested in the
share adult concerns with their subjects. In 1973
paper which argued that children were a 'muted
anthropologists and given no voice in the anthro-
hat children deserved to be studied in their own
*lture*, their own network of relationships, their own
ually more and more anthropologists have turned
the lives of children. This has been important for
lowing reasons:

not just as developing adults or adults-to-be, but as

not just in their families or at school, but in their
action with other children and with adults both
group.

**Fig. 27** Toshiro Mifune and Kyoko Kagawa in *High and Low* (Kurosawa, 1963).

depiction of social institutions and practices of the time than for their storylines. *I Live in Fear* was at one point intended to be a satire,[5] but the studio felt that the subject matter was too controversial, which is too bad, because the film simply takes itself far too seriously.

In *Scandal* Mifune plays a motorcycle-riding, pipe-smoking artist who is caught up in a tabloid scandal with a singer played by "Shirley" (Yoshiku) Yamaguchi. What starts out as a muckraking critique of the press, with a romance between highflying celebrities, soon degenerates into a maudlin story about a guilt-ridden lawyer played by Takashi Shimura. As Galbraith points out, there is a bit too much Frank Capra in this enthusiastic embrace of American film,[6] although the Shimura role is subsequently developed in *Ikiru*, one of Kurosawa's finest films. The two very different stories in *Scandal* represent a certain tension between Kurosawa's two main actors, Mifune and Shimura, which in so many other films is a productive acting team.

Takashi Shimura appears in 23 of Kurosawa's films, and virtually every single one from *Sanshiro Sugata* in 1943 to *Red Beard* in 1965. While his starring role in *Ikiru* is perhaps the most memorable, Shimura also plays the woodcutter in *Rashomon* and Kambei, the head samurai, in *Seven Samurai*. In *Drunken Angel*, *The Quiet Duel* (1949), *Stray Dog*, *Scandal* and *Seven Samurai*, Shimura plays the paternal *sensei* figure — doctor, lawyer or police inspector — to Mifune's angry young man. Their relationship is much the same in *I Live in Fear* as, despite Mifune's character's age, he is as unreasonable as his "young buck" characters in the other films. Thus Mifune's reconfiguration of Japanese masculinity tends to be carefully overseen, if not managed, by Shimura's companion roles of compassionate father figures. He may be half Mifune's height, but he provides a certain rock-solid anchoring effect that balances the younger man's movement-based performance style.

**Fig. 28** Takashi Shimura and Toshiro Mifune in *Stray Dog* (Kurosawa, 1949).

In many other films, one has to squint to find Shimura within the groups of men that circulate around Mifune. But there he is, in *Throne of Blood* and *The Bad Sleep Well*, playing secondary characters, along with a number of other key actors who appear over and over again. In all the enthusiasm over Mifune, the rest of Kurosawa's stable of actors tend to get overlooked. Minoru Chiaki and Kamatari Fujiwara, for example, the two rascals in *The Hidden Fortress*, can be found in quite a few films. Chiaki plays one of the seven samurai, the priest in *Rashomon*, and Mifune's pal in *Throne of Blood* (the Banquo character in this adaptation of *Macbeth*). Fujiwara, a Toho stalwart, appears in every film from *Ikiru* to *Kagemusha*. Before Mifune, Susumu Fujita played the judo-wrestling protagonist in both parts of *Sanshiro Sugata* (1943, 1945) (with Shimura as the paternal figure in part one), and also had leading roles in *The Men Who Tread on the Tiger's Tail* and *No Regrets for Our Youth*. The detail that Galbraith's book provides on these and other members of the Kurosawa-*kumi* (the production team) provides a fascinating insight into how the director was reliant on, and supported by, the structures and practices of the Japanese film industry and its star system. In one of Kurosawa's first films, it was the popular comedian Enoken who had star status as the porter-cum-guide in *Tiger's Tail*.

In his films of the 1980s Kurosawa turned to the stage-trained actor Tatsuya Nakadai to play the lead in both *Kagemusha* and *Ran*. Nakadai first appears in a Kurosawa film as Mifune's final opponent in *Yojimbo* and then in *Sanjuro*.

**Fig. 29** Misa Uehara, Toshiro Mifune, Minoru Chiaki and Kamatari Fujiwara in *The Hidden Fortress* (Kurosawa, 1958).

While Mifune claims that he was "too busy" to appear in the later films, other reports suggest that he was never asked. Nakadai says the director wanted a more internalized interpretation than the movement-based style of Mifune, although he ends up with just as few close-ups as Mifune ever got, if not fewer. Galbraith teases the reader with an explanation for the falling-out between Kurosawa and Mifune after *Red Beard*, their last film together. But in the end there doesn't seem to be any single explanation for their estrangement other than the pressures of the industry. As Kurosawa struggled to find financial backing for his increasingly expensive productions, Mifune worked hard to keep his own production company afloat.

When Toho radically scaled down its production schedule in 1963, Mifune chose to start his own production company. He only directed one film, *Legacy of the 500000* (1964), but went on to produce 12 more that he also starred in, including Kobayashi's *Samurai Rebellion* (1967). After *Yojimbo*, Mifune became a global star, acting in a dozen international productions such as *Grand Prix* (Frankenheimer, 1966), *Hell in the Pacific* (Boorman, 1968), *1941* (Spielberg, 1979), *Shogun* (Jerry London, 1980) and *The Challenge* (Frankenheimer, 1982). Galbraith goes into excruciating detail on many of the titles in Mifune's 117-film filmography, and his book provides a rare look at the Japanese action genres that Mifune starred in. His tough-guy image more or less provided the foundation of the postwar samurai film genre, as films like the Miyamoto Musashi series (1955–56) were hugely popular in Japan. Mifune also appeared in dozens of war films as the Japanese rehashed the Pacific War throughout the 1950s and 1960s.

It is not unreasonable to suppose that Mifune simply became "too busy" to act in Kurosawa's films, which often took months of planning, rehearsing and shooting. Galbraith suggests that Mifune needed an extended vacation from Kurosawa after *Red Beard*, for which he had taken valuable time away from his own company.[7] It is also true that in *Red Beard* Mifune starred opposite Yuzo Kayama, a rising star who plays the apprentice to Mifune's *sensei*, the role that would have been given to Shimura in the past. By 1965, Mifune was no longer a young man and, even with his international reputation, he could not provide the bankability that Kurosawa needed in a collapsing industry. Kurosawa floundered after *Red Beard*. He made only seven more films between 1970 and 1993, whereas he had made 24 films between 1943 and 1965.

**Fig. 30** Yuzo Kayama and Toshiro Mifune in *Red Beard* (Kurosawa, 1965).

## TECHNIQUE

George Lucas introduces the DVD of *The Hidden Fortress* by praising Kurosawa's use of long lenses. Robert Altman is interviewed on the *Rashomon* disk, praising Kurosawa's storytelling technique and he is very articulate about what others have called "the *Rashomon* effect." Although these films do not need the Hollywood accreditation, it is interesting to think that Kurosawa's film might have influenced Altman's favored "network narrative" film structure. Adam Low's documentary provides substantial testimony about Kurosawa's technique from interviews with a number of key actors, including Nakadai, Isuzu Yamada and Machiko Kyo, and key members of the Kurosawa-*kumi*, including Kurosawa's daughter Kazuko, script supervisor Teruyo Nogami, scriptwriter Shinobu Hashimoto, production designer Yoshiro Muraki and cameraman Takao Saito. *Kurosawa* is supplemented by additional interview footage, probably culled from the Toho Masterwork's series.

The highlight for me of all the additional material included on the DVDs is an excerpt from an NHK documentary on Kazuo Miyagawa included on the *Rashomon* disk. Miyagawa is the cameraman who is most closely associated with Mizoguchi, and he worked for Daiei where Kurosawa made *Rashomon*. Going into the production, Miyagawa says, he wanted to impress the director and surprise him on the first day of shooting. The two men had pretty big reputations and were from different studios, so there was a spirit of competitiveness that infected their collaboration in the best way possible. The NHK documentary includes a schematic diagram of how Miyagawa shot the woodcutter's walk through the forest by having the actor — Takashi Shimura — cross the dolly tracks laid on the forest floor. It is only one moment in a virtuoso film in which Miyagawa also used mirrors and lots of foliage-waving to create that famous dappled effect of the ambiguous events in the grove. For Altman the revelation of *Rashomon* was that four versions of the same story proved to him that "it is all true and none of it is true," which suggested to him what is possible with film. But the *Rashomon* effect is not merely a question of scriptwriting and narrative structure; it has a great deal to do with the film's visual style.

**Fig. 31** Takashi Shimura in *Rashomon* (Kurosawa, 1950).

One of the oft-repeated tag lines about Kurosawa, which like so much of Galbraith's book and Low's documentary originates in Kurosawa's *Something Like an Autobiography* (1982), is that he was primordially influenced by silent film. The use of visual style, and the ability to create powerful cinematic effects with a minimal degree of technology is what makes Kurosawa a modernist. His predilection for long lenses creates a shallow depth of field in which composition within the frame is paramount. Add to that his use of multiple moving cameras, introduced with *Seven Samurai*, and you have the basis of the dynamic kinetic effect of so many of the films. While the editing of the *chambara* is notoriously rapid-fire, it only works because it is juxtaposed with much slower sequences. Next to Mifune's dramatic death scene in *Throne of Blood*, the most repeated scene in Low's documentary (replayed on the little viewers) is the slow-motion collapse of a samurai killed by a single sword thrust in a field of grass in *Seven Samurai*.

**Fig. 32** Toshiro Mifune in *Throne of Blood* (Kurosawa, 1957).

This is a director who was not afraid to use fast motion, slow motion or extreme high or low angles. He turns off the soundtrack altogether for a moment in *Ikiru*, and in *High and Low* throws a dash of color into a black-and-white film. He may not be as far off the codes of continuity editing as his contemporary Yasujiro Ozu, but he is never afraid to break the rules to produce the effects he's looking for. While he sometimes falls for the worst clichés of Western music, the burst of jazz music in the middle of *Sanjuro* is a stroke of genius. Fumio Hayasaka, who scored the Ravel-inspired *Rashomon* and seven other titles, including *Seven Samurai*, was succeeded by his student Masaru Sato, who was responsible for the dynamic jazz motifs in *Yojimbo* and *Sanjuro* and the 1960s *gendai-geki High and Low* and *The Bad Sleep Well*, as well as composing for the more traditional instrumentation of *Throne of Blood*.

Kurosawa's signature visual device is the wipe-cut. It appears in his first film *Sanshiro Sugata* and it is especially prominent in *The Men Who Tread on the Tiger's Tail*, where it is used extensively as an editing device within scenes and sequences; not just between scenes, as it functions in later films. As Yoshimoto has pointed out, in this early film, an adaptation of a *kabuki* classic, Kurosawa was working toward a Japanese cinema that would be free of the trappings of classical theater. The hard-edged wipe is a technique that foregrounds the compositional aspects of the image; it renders the frame two-dimensional and flat, radically inscribing the photographic properties of the cinema onto a script and performance style that, in *Tiger's Tail*, were drawn from theater. Kurosawa continued to use the device throughout his career, up to and including *Ran*, and it is an important element of his cinema.

For Gilles Deleuze, Kurosawa's wipe-cut represents the "breath that animates the void"; it has a unifying effect even while it takes all the depth from the image.[8] The director's signature stroke joins the "great circle of humanism" by which he links highs and lows, rich and poor. I'll come back to Kurosawa's humanist ideology shortly, but the wipe-cut, as a signature, is what marks his indebtedness to the aesthetics of silent film and the principles of montage established by Sergei Eisenstein — which are of course themselves indebted to the pictorial arts of China and Japan. In one of the added interviews on the documentary disk, Mitsuhiro Shinoda describes the timing and musicality of Kurosawa's wipe-cuts and how thrilling they were to him as a young filmmaker. He points out that Kurosawa shot and edited as he went along, going back for retakes immediately and easily whenever he needed them. His multiple-moving-camera technique gave him many different angles and lenses for any given scene, which were then edited together to create what Shinoda calls a three-dimensional quality. Given his extensive use of long lenses, this depth is achieved through montage, not through focal length.

It is not surprising that Kurosawa chafed under Hollywood production methods. His distinctive style was really made possible by the small scale of the Japanese industry and his ability to work with a regular crew or *kumi* who accommodated both his idiosyncrasies and his notorious authoritarian style. His nickname on the set was "the Emperor" (whereas Mifune comes across in

Galbraith's book as a kindhearted soul who was never too proud to serve tea to his crew). Kurosawa also pushed the small industry to its limits, making huge demands on Toho's staff and coffers. For the ransom drop-off scene in *High and Low*, for example, he commandeered every single camera and operator on the Toho lot to catch the tossing of the briefcase out the window of a Shinkansen train crossing a bridge over a ravine.[9]

## MEN ON HORSES

Kurosawa's films are sometimes referred to as "Japanese westerns," a term that may help to pinpoint his unyielding emphasis on masculinity and the relations between men, but is woefully inaccurate on almost every other level. True enough, one can find quite a few moments in his films that evoke John Ford's westerns. The horseback scenes in *The Hidden Fortress* and *Seven Samurai*, lines of horsemen appearing over hilltops in *Throne of Blood* and *Ran*, the guys singing around a campfire in *Dersu Uzala* (1975); all of this iconography paves the way for Mifune's status as the Japanese "Duke." And yet, Kurosawa has a fundamentally different approach to landscape and space than one finds in the American western and his historical references are to a very different society. As there is no "frontier" in Japan this should not be too surprising, but Kurosawa goes further in closing off the openness of landscape than perhaps any other director. His famous use of rain, for example, and the incredible fog in *Throne of Blood*; mist, snow, high winds and gallons and gallons of rain have the effect of flattening the image in yet another way and rendering it two-dimensional. The landscape in *The Hidden Fortress* is dominated by rocky barrens that surround the action like an amphitheater. Kurosawa is much more preoccupied with foreground objects than background vistas, which only occasionally appear in the frame. His long lenses render the spectacular countryside of *Ran* as distant shadows behind the foreground figures. Typical is the most famous closing shot of that film, a two-dimensional silhouette of a man on a cliff.

Exceptions to this principle can be found in a few films, but these are not the so-called Japanese westerns. The subarctic landscape of *Dersu Uzala* is, indeed, a frontier land. One wishes that Kurosawa had found a way of developing the script beyond the tired formula of the mountain-man saga. *Dreams* (1990) may also be considered as a landscape film, but in this case the ersatz vistas

**Fig. 33** Misa Uehara in *The Hidden Fortress* (Kurosawa, 1958).

are so busily "painterly" they are completely lacking in depth. One of the most moving uses of expansive space can be found at the end of *Kagemusha* as the decommissioned shadow warrior wanders among the corpses of his fallen companions. This image, like the battle scenes in *Ran*, is curiously evocative of the American Civil War repertoire of melancholy landscape.

If frontier landscape is not the holy grail of these "Japanese westerns," what is it that drives the narrative motor? I would suggest that in some films it is the transport and protection of noble bodies — precious people who need to be guarded. In *The Hidden Fortress* this is the princess Yuki; in *Kagemusha* it is the body of Shingen preserved in an urn, followed by the protection of the identity of his surrogate, the Kagemusha or shadow warrior; in *The Men Who Tread on the Tiger's Tail* the Lord Yoshitsune is smuggled across a border disguised as a porter. Kidnapping plots in *Sanjuro* and *High and Low* continue this theme of the valuable body. Given the divine status of the imperial body in Japanese history and politics, these tales of protection are very much in keeping with the national imaginary. For Kurosawa these bodies function as voids at the center of narratives that circulate around each hidden, silent precious person. In *Ran* the body of the father, Hidetora, fills a similar function, while his madness is yet another version of the imperial emptiness.

## MODERNISM/HUMANISM

The forest of *Rashomon* is emblematic of Kurosawa's closed-in natural environment. The grove is at once a room, a stage and a labyrinth, but equally important in that film is the Zen garden courtroom where the protagonists confess their various versions of the tragic and erotic events of the grove. This set is exemplary of the minimalist architecture that Kurosawa uses so well in both the *jidai-geki* sets of *Red Beard, Kagemusha* and *Throne of Blood* and the modernist architecture of *High and Low*. In the latter film one can see how Japanese modernity can be so closely linked to traditional aesthetics. Space in Kurosawa is not organized around point of view, but around social relations and the divisions among people.

*Rashomon* is the only one of Kurosawa's films that embraces the void, the nothingness behind social hierarchies and the fiction behind the image. But even *Rashomon* falters in the end over the *deus ex machina* of a foundling child. Morality is restored to a broken world. As with *Seven Samurai*, the allusion to postwar Japan is not hard to read, and both films serve as powerful national allegories. After 5 years of American occupation in which the cultural values of the previous 15 were rigorously reversed, the ambiguities, deceptions and doubts of *Rashomon* are extremely pertinent, and its ending constitutes a kind of desperate optimism, even if the film itself was not immediately appreciated in Japanese theaters. Likewise, the renunciation of military values becomes allegorically reconfigured as the death of noble samurai fighting for a good cause in *Seven Samurai*. Kurosawa's capacity as a mythmaker is what finally seals his pact with John Ford.

Deleuze suggests that it may be D. W. Griffith with whom Kurosawa shares the most,[10] which is an interesting proposition, and in tune with his use of American Civil War iconography. It is not just because of Kurosawa's visual style but also his humanist ideology that he shares with Griffith. The reassembled ronin of *Seven Samurai* are fighting for the poor farmers; and the businessman pays the ransom for the chauffeur's child in *High and Low*. In film after film, great men find ways to be compassionate to other, "lesser" men. The two clowns in *The Hidden Fortress* are finally rewarded, but the premise of this film, as with *The Lower Depths* (1957), *Dersu Uzala, High and Low* and *Red Beard*, is that there are absolute divisions among men that can be bridged by compassion, but are otherwise irrevocable. In films set within the "feudal" society of the Japanese past, this is of course a given, although the iconography of the "lowly" feeds Kurosawa's ideology of humanism as strongly as his construction of heroism. From the dank swamp of *Drunken Angel* to the crowded tenement of *The Lower Depths*, the heroin galleries of *High and Low*, the garbage-dump set of *Dodes'kaden* (1970), and the black-market neighborhoods of *Stray Dog*, Kurosawa visualizes the underclasses as filthy, grotesque and melancholy.

We cannot position Kurosawa as either a modernist or a humanist, as these terms have such shifting meanings within a global cultural milieu. His humanism may be a modern modality in Japan, a more democratic and just mode of storytelling and depiction of class relations; yet it also falls victim to many of the clichés of Western humanism. Kurosawa's storytelling and filmmaking technique is so highly fragmented and nonlinear, so reflexive and experimental that his modernity may be aligned with the most radical of cineastes. And yet, he is very much a "realist," given the meticulous detailed research that goes into his sets and costume design. This is something that comes across even more clearly in the remastered digital releases of the film: the card catalogs in *Stray Dog*, for example, which the Toho art department carefully constructed by actually writing out the contents of the cards in the police department drawers. This level of detail, which is pervasive in both the *jidai-geki* and the *gendai-geki*, aligns Kurosawa with American melodramatists such as D. W. Griffith and Vincente Minnelli, for whom detailed backgrounds and extreme weather conditions are key components of narrative meaning.

**Fig. 34** Reikichi Kawamura and Toshiro Mifune in *Stray Dog* (Kurosawa, 1949).

## KUROSAWA'S WOMEN

Where Kurosawa's humanism stumbles most awkwardly is in his depiction of women, who remain as "other" as the poor and downtrodden. His most avowedly pro-democracy film *No Regrets for Our Youth*, which features the strongest female protagonist in his oeuvre, played by Setsuko Hara, fails miserably to follow through on its promise of female emancipation. Hara's character, Yukie, moves through the film from university student and passionate pianist to becoming a bourgeois housewife to a dutiful daughter-in-law plowing the muck in torrents of bad weather. Like many films of this period, it is an attempt to comply with the Occupation mandate to feature female protagonists, without endowing the female characters with any coherent subjectivity. *One Wonderful Sunday* (1947) is ostensibly about a couple more or less wandering through a bad date in the ruined and rebuilding city of 1947, but the woman is a mere spectator to her suitor's final fantasy of conducting Schubert in an empty auditorium — until she mounts the stage for the big kiss (another activity mandated by the SCAP [Supreme Commander of Allied Powers] script patrol).

**Fig. 35**   Setsuko Hara in *No Regrets for Our Youth* (Kurosawa, 1946).

Other female characters tend to be either meek and mild love interests or wives, or femme fatales prone to hysterics (*Throne of Blood, Rashomon, Red Beard, Ran*). To be sure, the great actresses Isuzu Yamada, Haruko Sugimura, Machiko Kyo and Mieko Harada all have some great scenes, but their roles are far too small. Ironically, the trailer for *Ran*, included on the Fox DVD, contains four scenes of women, all violently erotic, far out of proportion to the screen time given to women in the film itself. In adapting *King Lear*, Kurosawa not only changed the three daughters to three sons but also converted the Edmund figure to a violent femme fatale avenging a violent past. Kyoko Kagawa appeared in five of his films and admits that her character in *The Bad Sleep Well*, the crippled wife Keiko, did not express herself at all, which made it a very difficult role to play. Indeed, this woman is nothing but a pawn in a game between men, her marriage nothing but a vehicle for the Mifune character's revenge on her family.

In two films women are included in the family groups that structure the visible field — *The Idiot* (1951) and *I Live in Fear* — but, again, none of them are given convincing or full-fledged characterizations. On the other hand, Kurosawa's direction of Setsuko Hara in *No Regrets for Our Youth* and *The Idiot* actually challenges the actress in ways that Ozu never attempted. Unfortunately, in both cases her performance was roundly chastised by the critical community. In the former she was accused of being "monstrous" and in the latter, of overacting, criticisms that are perhaps generated by the contradictory scripts of those films and don't give Kurosawa enough credit for trying to push Hara beyond the demure maiden role that she was doomed to devote her career to as Japan's "eternal virgin."

Keiko Awaji's discussion of her performance in *Stray Dog* is somewhat illuminating of Kurosawa's method. She claims that she did not want to act in movies but she was selected by Toho from an operetta company and persuaded to take the role. She was unhappy throughout the shoot and her sulky sullenness becomes the articulation of a character reluctant to cooperate with the authorities. She talked back to the director and slouched and pouted her way through the film. The result is a fresh new look, a kind of insolence that indicated a new woman of the postwar generation.

## IKIRU

The only really interesting female character in Kurosawa's entire cinema is Toyo Odagiri (played by Miki Odagiri in her only major screen role) in *Ikiru*. She is the only woman who seems to be able to exist outside the family system. Her free spirit provides the inspiration for Watanabe (the Shimura character) to lift himself out of the bureaucratic mire and do a good deed for the community. *Ikiru* is my favorite of Kurosawa's films, and not only because it eschews the absolute class divisions that underscore the "humanism" of so many of the other films. In *Ikiru* the two-part narrative structure that systematically runs

**Fig. 36** Miki Odagiri in *Ikiru* (Kurosawa, 1952).

through his scriptwriting is most perfectly foregrounded. Watanabe's death halfway through the film opens onto an epilogue in which the story of his last days is pieced together from the drunken confessions of his former colleagues — another group of men.

*Ikiru* is the first film that Kurosawa collaborated on with screenwriter Hideo Oguni, who reportedly devised the two-part structure. The two parts of Kurosawa's scripts are not plot and subplot; nor are they always exposition followed by action, although that is certainly the case in *Seven Samurai* and *High and Low*. Even before working with Oguni, Kurosawa had written *Rashomon*, a script with distinct sections, with another long-time collaborator, Shinobu Hashimoto. In many of these films the different parts correspond to distinct spatial arrangements, as in the descent to the city from the hilltop in *High and Low*. When Kurosawa departs from this structure, either by adapting a work that lacks it — as in *The Lower Depths* — or when he moves to a serial format as with *Dreams*, everything falls apart. Deleuze suggests that in Kurosawa's worldview the hero must have all the "givens" laid out before him and then he can act. The different parts of the script thus construct a theatrical space that Deleuze describes as "contracted," and, again, *Ikiru* must be the best example of this.[11] Except that in *Ikiru*, as in *Rashomon*, the heroic action is retold by others, and performed in flashback.

Screenwriting was in many ways Kurosawa's premier creative activity, and he wrote many more scripts than he himself produced. It was his ticket into

**Fig. 37** Takashi Shimura in *Ikiru* (Kurosawa, 1952).

the studio hierarchy, enabling him to be promoted at a young age. In his long discussion with Oshima, Kurosawa stresses the necessity for good filmmakers to be good writers. Even so, it is evident that his own scripts were highly collaborative and, like many productions of the period, they tended to involve long retreats in the country where high levels of productivity and brainstorming were fueled by alcohol.

## THE CITY

*Ikiru* is also an important film in Kurosawa's cinema because it deals directly with the issue of urban development. Watanabe's existential quest is set against the landscape of postwar Tokyo, a city that experienced a rapid sprawl of accelerated growth in the 1950s. Several of Kurosawa's *gendai-geki* are set in the milieu of the postwar metropolis, employing crime-fiction narratives to explore the hidden vice dens, transportation networks and suburban wastelands. In *One Wonderful Sunday* and *Stray Dog*, he uses documentary methods to bind the fiction to the city; in *High and Low* and *The Bad Sleep Well* he employs the full repertoire of noir iconography — cars, phones, mirrors, newspaper headlines, guns and photographs. The wedding cake in the latter film, sculpted into an office building and served up with a rose marking the scene of a crime, is one of the most memorable images of Kurosawa's cinema. Sato's jazzy soundtrack to *The Bad Sleep Well* is one of the most dynamic of his career.

**Fig. 38** *The Bad Sleep Well* (Kurosawa, 1960).

*Ikiru* also features a famous nightclub sequence as Watanabe follows his Mephistopheles through the burlesque parlors and jazz clubs of a thoroughly Americanized Tokyo. Similar scenes in *Stray Dog* and *Drunken Angel* feature female performers and well-dressed gangsters, and the characters indulge themselves in singing and dancing. While these pleasure quarters are heavily laden with moral censure they are also incredibly lively and dynamic scenes, suggesting how the sensuality of American culture triggered a real break with the authoritarian norms of Japanese culture. These are democratic pleasures, productions of a mass culture that knows no borders. In the temptations that confront Watanabe one can easily glimpse the modernity that Kurosawa's cinema adapted in so many ways to Japanese visual culture. In these city films the hierarchies of people still exist to be sure, and the paternalistic family system remains in place despite the rampant crime, disease, violence and sexuality. However, one can also see how the social order is challenged by the introduction of new subjectivities in postwar Japan.

The men in the city films may be wearing suits but they are usually rumpled and drenched with sweat. Kurosawa's preoccupation with weather goes beyond visual effects to the creation of sensuous environments, such as the mud in *Seven Samurai*, and the extreme heat that oppresses the characters in *Stray Dog*, *I Live in Fear* and *High and Low*. The "realism" of Kurosawa's cinema is usually identified with his painstaking historical detail, such as the accuracy of his samurai costuming, and the medical paraphernalia of *Red Beard*, but it is equally a realism of effect. The extreme weather conditions that appear in virtually every film give tangible form to the characters' various trials and tribulations. In the city films, they soften the urban setting into a site of humanist compassion, exemplified by the final soft snowfall of *Ikiru*.

## SPECTACLE

The city films are no less spectacular than the *jidai-geki*, often using evocative urban settings like the abandoned munitions factory in *The Bad Sleep Well* and the Yokohama cityscape in *High and Low*. Kurosawa first used CinemaScope — or Tohoscope — in 1958 with *The Hidden Fortress*. By then it had been adopted widely within the Japanese industry, for much the same reasons as it was in the United States — as a means of differentiating movies from the threat of television. Now that the TV vs. film debate has supposedly dissolved into properly formatted DVDs, Kurosawa's widescreen films still need a big screen to be fully appreciated. *Kagemusha* and *Ran*, shot in a slightly narrower Vistavision format, also need a big screen for their spectacular production designs. Kurosawa's six Scope features, made from 1958 to 1965, constitute extraordinary uses of the widescreen format. For Stephen Prince, the Scope frame is the third ingredient — added to the long lenses and multiple-moving-camera filming — in Kurosawa's mature style.[12] Like many of his contemporaries, such as Ichikawa, Imamura, Naruse and Oshima, he exploits the compositional properties of the format, using diagonals and sectioning the frame with interior architecture. In *High and Low* he blocks the groups of men among the huge modern furniture like figures in a landscape. In *Yojimbo* and *Sanjuro*, Mifune's great swordplay scenes are choreographed within the rectangular frame that captures the quick horizontal movement of bodies and weapons.

The spectacular qualities of Kurosawa's cinema are, of course, bound up with his aesthetics of violence. The big battle scenes of *Seven Samurai*, *Kagemusha* and *Ran*; Mifune's samurai character slashing his way through dozens of men at a time; the knife-wielding women of *Throne of Blood*, *Red Beard* and *Ran*, and the knife and pistol duels of *Drunken Angel* and *Stray Dog* — in all of these

**Fig. 39** Toshiro Mifune in *High and Low* (Kurosawa, 1963).

he uses inventive stylistic effects that have entered into the vocabulary of the action film, the thriller and the horror film. Mifune's death scene in *Throne of Blood* is only one of many in Kurosawa's cinema, although its dramatic excess may be matched only by Mifune's spectacular death scene in *Drunken Angel*, in which he ends up dangling upside down from a tenement balcony after crawling through a couple of long hallways covered in white paint and blood.

In *Yojimbo* Kurosawa began using the sound of meat being slashed to accompany the swordplay; in *Sanjuro*, the first gushing spurt of blood was accidentally produced by a nervous assistant. In addition to these graphic effects, the director also uses more oblique effects, like the huge bloodstain on the wall that haunts the Cobweb Castle in *Throne of Blood*, and which marks the death of the villainess in *Ran*. The violent action is like the wipe-cut: fast and straight-edged. The signature vertical line radically separates different spaces and times, as the slash of a sword separates life and death, not to mention limbs from bodies. The void is never far away, and Kurosawa's aesthetics of violence are apiece with his stylized visual field.

*Ran* is the late film in which all the thematics and stylistic effects are reconstituted for the last time. It is also Kurosawa's most successful use of a theatrical color palette, something he tried in *Dodes'kaden* and *Dreams* with disappointing results. He avoided color photography until 1970, and only in *Dersu Uzala* does he exploit its realist properties. In the other late films it becomes a key ingredient in his development of a fantasy world. To the extent that *The Hidden Fortress* influenced George Lucas, *Ran* is a post–*Star Wars* landscape of brightly colored and costumed figures. Kurosawa started experimenting with fantasy-like dream sequences as early as *Drunken Angel*, and in numerous instances blurs reality and fantasy with the introduction of supernatural figures. Although it may be true that the costumes and sets of *Ran* represent a carefully researched historical accuracy, the bold primary colors also belong to the idealized realm of the fantastic.

## THE LATE CAREER

The fiasco of *Tora! Tora! Tora!* in 1967, Kurosawa's most infamous flirtation with Hollywood, was preceded by another unfinished project called *Runaway Train* in 1966. He put considerable time and effort into both projects before backing out under adverse circumstances. Galbraith explains that much of Kurosawa's difficulties with these failed projects was due to corruption within his own company. One of his most trusted associates, Tetsu Aoyagi, the son of one of Kurosawa's close friends, had mislead the director and his production company, and badly mismanaged the picture deals that he set up with the Americans. As Galbraith points out, it's a story right out of the movies, particularly echoing Kurosawa's *The Bad Sleep Well*.

Kurosawa had established his own production company in 1959, working in association with Toho until 1970 when he went completely independent with *Dodes'kaden*. The financial disaster of that production squashed any further projects by the short-lived "Club of Four Knights" (which included Kon Ichikawa, Keisuke Kinoshita and Masaki Kobayashi along with Kurosawa), for whom it became their only completed film. After *Dodes'kaden*, Kurosawa was entirely dependent on foreign investment. Fortunately, by the 1970s his technical virtuosity was appreciated by the new breed of American film school–trained directors and European producers such as Mosfilm, which produced *Dersu Uzala* in 1975 (Roger Corman produced the US version), and Serge Silberman, who produced *Ran* in 1985 out of Paris.

By 1985 Kurosawa had outlived many of his *kumi* members, but managed, nevertheless, to reinvent many devices with new collaborators. "Peter" who plays the fool in *Ran*, was a popular TV drag star and avant-garde film actor, and in many ways is a harking back to Enoken, providing that key element of satire that lifts films like *Yojimbo* and *Sanjuro* out of the sentimentality that so often plagues Kurosawa's scripts. The excellent score for *Ran* is composed by one of Japan's great film composers, Toru Takemitsu, as by now Kurosawa had had a final falling-out with Masaru Sato. Takemitsu's subtle use of Japanese instrumentation and Western classical symphonic music is badly lacking in *Kagemusha*, which has one of the worst scores of the director's entire oeuvre. In both *Kagemusha* and *Ran* Kurosawa relied on one of his few long-standing colleagues from Toho, Ishiro Honda, a chief assistant director. Honda, the director of Toho's *Godzilla* series, had a long friendship with Kurosawa, having started their careers together at Toho in the 1930s as assistant directors, and he was one of Kurosawa's most important collaborators in the last phase of his career.

The Japanese industry inexplicably overlooked *Ran* in its selection for the

Academy Awards in 1985. Kurosawa had already won an award for best foreign film in 1976 for *Dersu Uzala*, although it was entered as a Soviet film. (He won an honorary Oscar in 1990.) The rejection of *Ran* by the Japanese industry and critical establishment capped off a career of antagonism between Kurosawa and the industry. Throughout his career Kurosawa experienced a certain resentment and rejection by his countrymen for allegedly pandering to Western tastes. It is difficult to assess the real degree and extent of this antagonism, as his films continued to win prizes and rank highly on the *Kinema Junpo* top-ten lists right up to and including his last film, *Madadayo*.

The cruelties of the Japanese industry are perhaps best represented by the whiskey commercials that Kurosawa was persuaded to make in 1976. Included in Low's documentary, the director wears his trademark sunglasses, perched against a rural landscape, glumly sipping from a huge tumbler (subsequently satirized by Bill Murray in *Lost in Translation* [Sofia Coppola, 2003]). Mifune also made a beer commercial in 1970, with the slogan "Real men just drink, without saying a word." Both actor and director needed to trade in on their tough-guy images in the 1970s as the industry nosedived and their own companies were plagued by corruption. These ads are indicative of how closely tied their names were to mass culture and also how, in their own films together, they helped to develop a mass culture that would be fundamentally different from that imported from abroad.

Kurosawa's cultural currency may have been at its lowest ebb in Japan in the early 1970s. Cut off by the studios who could no longer afford him, he was also chastised by the new generation of "New Wave" directors. Kurosawa's "simplistic humanism" was denounced by Shinoda, his engagement with traditional genres was criticized by Oshima as a forced Japaneseness, and Terayama thought him too classical. And yet, in so many ways, it is his cinema that paves the way for the political cinema of the 1960s. He developed a visual style appropriate to a cinema of conflict and violence, which of course became the dominant mode of the generation that scorned him. Because his was the cinema most widely exported outside Japan, it became identified with a national cinema, the terms of which began to be seriously interrogated during the 1960s.

Kurosawa had no better luck with American critics than he did with the Japanese. Galbraith summarizes the American critical reception of each of the films and, while there are certainly some enthusiastic and observant writers among them (Galbraith singles out Arthur Knight in particular),[13] the recurring theme is an Orientalist complaint that Kurosawa simply copies from Western cultural forms. If he isn't copying outright, then the films may have some merit as exotic novelties, but rarely are they taken on their own terms. It has taken over 50 years for the critical establishment to get over the Japanese-Western binaries that has plagued Kurosawa criticism. His cinema in fact forces us to understand and recognize the visual vocabulary and thematic concerns of Japanese modernity.

Japanese film studies has been perpetually hung up on auteurism, but while it is true that authorship is a structural feature of the Japanese industry, the lit-crit approach is notoriously ill-equipped to deal with the full scope of the work of a studio-based director like Kurosawa who was committed equally to entertainment and art cinema. His cinema is incredibly uneven and inconsistent and in many instances demands more of a cultural studies approach. And yet, even some of his most maligned films contain surprises, especially if they are not approached as "Kurosawa" films but as cultural artifacts of one of the world's largest cinemas. For example, the 1951 film *The Idiot*, an adaptation of the Dostoevsky novel set in postwar Hokkaido, is supposedly one of the director's big embarrassments. The close-up cinematography in the film, however, is absolutely stunning. The final soft-focus embrace between Mifune and Masayuki Mori certainly doesn't fit the image of the "warrior's cinema," nor is it consistent with the director's dominant style, but it is really the only opportunity Kurosawa ever offers to study the beautiful face of Toshiro Mifune. In fact, the attempt to transpose the drama of fallen aristocracy to the Japanese context is not as absurd as it seems, and it enables Kurosawa to approach his emblematic subject of masculinity in a fresh way.

On the other hand, the less said about the last two films, *Rhapsody in August* (1991) and *Madadayo* (1993), the better. Both films return to the war, but the efforts to link present and past founder on sentimental clichés. As children and the elderly take center stage in these late films, Kurosawa seems unable or unwilling to confront contemporary Japanese society. Whereas *Yojimbo* thrilled audiences equally in Japan and the United States during 1961, it is *Red Beard*, according to Galbraith, that remains Kurosawa's most well-known and popular film in Japan.[14] The technical perfection of *Red Beard* may be Kurosawa's ultimate expression of "humanism" for some, but, as Yoshimoto suggests, it may

**Fig. 40** Toshiro Mifune and Masayuki Mori in *The Idiot* (Kurosawa, 1951).

be "too perfect," lacking any narrative or aesthetic conflict or ambiguity.[15] Its didactic tone and patriarchal authoritarianism are somewhat overwhelming. And yet this may be the unspoken truth that sustains the director's so-called humanist worldview.

International audiences prefer that they be unsettled by the kinetic visual style that in *Red Beard* becomes a static formalism. The theatrical trailer included on the *Red Beard* DVD indicates how, even by 1965, Kurosawa's cinema was becoming out of synch with the times. Breaking the film down into cryptic and epigrammatic phrases, the trailer concludes with shots of the audio recording technology actively taping the score being played by a studio orchestra. In contrast to the avant-garde features of the (uncredited) trailer, the film itself is a highly linear, closed text. For some Japanese audiences, the unambiguous statement of paternalist ideology in *Red Beard* may finally align Kurosawa with a "classical" cinema espousing the "Japaneseness" that otherwise seems to elude him. But Japanese audiences are as diverse as North American audiences, and one can also understand how the radical filmmakers of the day associated him with a tired style that they were set on dismantling.

The institutionalized distinction between *jidai-geki* and *gendai-geki* does not mean that Kurosawa's samurai are stuck in the past, and it certainly doesn't mean that his guys with ties are "Westernized" men. In his cinema we can see how the two genres are intimately related. Questions of heroism, individual action, willpower and compassion are framed again and again against assemblies of groups of men, framed as blocks of figures. The background may be a large or small *tatami* room; it may be a wide village street; or it may be a battlefield. But the background will always be a little bit blurry, a sketchy afterthought to the bold design of the foreground figures, much like the subservient roles of women in Kurosawa's scripts. This is, in the end, a macho cinema that may not be afraid to cry, but is never afraid to take risks.

*Chapter Five*

# Mikio Naruse: A Japanese Woman's Cinema

The long career of Mikio Naruse provides many insights into classical Japanese cinema as a commercial industry and as a cultural practice. Naruse has long been recognized in Japan as the "number four" director, but it has taken many decades for his cinema to become widely known outside Japan. Although a few titles were in circulation in the 1980s and 1990s, thanks primarily to critic Audie Bock, the DVD releases have been slow to emerge. Naruse himself was not a self-promoter and his specialization in women's films may have helped to keep his work somewhat in the shadows. Moreover, his auteurist signature lacks the formal distinctiveness that one finds in Ozu, Mizoguchi and Kurosawa. In many ways, he adheres more closely to the Hollywood idiom than Orientalist critics are comfortable with.

As a studio director for 37 years, Naruse made 89 films, many of which received top prizes in the annual *Kinema Junpo* polls. He was very much a studio-based director, starting at Shochiku-Kamata in 1930 and moving to PCL in 1935 to begin making sound films. PCL was absorbed into Toho shortly thereafter and (with a few exceptions) Naruse remained with the studio until his final film, *Scattered Clouds*, in 1967. The studio environment meant that he worked with the same crew of writers, actors and camera, art direction and sound personnel for film after film. Several of his most popular films in the 1950s, including *Meshi* (1951) and *Floating Clouds* (1955), discussed here, were adapted from the writing of Fumiko Hayashi, one of the few woman writers to attain notoriety during this period.

The continuity of style that is evident in Naruse's cinema may be in part due to his network of collaborators, but we can also point to several recurring stylistic and narrative features. Until he began using widescreen in the late 1950s, he cut fairly quickly, often breaking continuity rules as Ozu did, but his lighting was more textured and the films display more of a realist aesthetic than one finds in Ozu's cinema, although the two directors both worked consistently in the *shoshimin-eiga* genre. Naruse's proclivity for women's stories meant that he worked with most of the big stars of the era, from whom he consistently drew outstanding performances. One of the most familiar traits of Naruse's films is the downcast eyes of a woman, expressing sadness, resignation or disappointment. And yet, his women characters are usually surprisingly resilient, strong-willed survivors. Typical also are "life-goes-on" endings in which not everything is resolved but the conditions for life to continue are restored. They are rarely conventional "happy endings," but are typically set on a road, a river or a bridge.

Naruse's silent films, of which only a handful have survived, are exuberant examples of the early 1930s city films, featuring young modern men and women, and a dynamic style of shooting and editing. He managed to work throughout the war and Occupation continuously, emerging in the early 1950s with a very strong series of "marriage films." Using the *shoshimin-eiga* genre framework, with its observational style of depicting everyday life in the lower middle classes, Naruse's marriage films dramatize the emotional and economic difficulties of couples attempting to make it on their own in the harsh conditions of the postwar era. Childless couples are featured in *Meshi* (a.k.a. *Repast*), *Tsuma* (*Wife*, 1953), *Fufu* (*Husband and Wife*, 1953), *Shuu* (*Sudden Rain*,1956), *Sound of the Mountain* (*Yama no oto*, 1954), *A Wife's Heart* (*Tsuma no kokoro*, 1956) and *Anzukko* (1958). In each of these films, the husband is a white-collar worker or "salaryman" near the bottom of a rigorous office hierarchy, and the women are bored housewives with little to do and not enough money to start a family.

While the marriage films paint a bleak picture of the limited options available to married women, another theme that Naruse developed was that of the geisha, the bar hostess or — in one of his best-known films of the 1950s, *Late Chrysanthemums* (*Bangiku*, 1954) — the lives of former geisha. The insight into this "women's world" was unique. His female characters in films like *Ginza Cosmetics* (*Ginza gesho*, 1951), *Flowing* (*Nagareru*, 1956) and *When a Woman Ascends the Stairs* (1960) are simply working women trying to get by; they are neither eroticized or exoticized, which was in itself a new way of depicting the *mizu shobai* or "water trade" in Japanese culture. All of Naruse's female characters are real, sympathetic, full-fledged characters, rather than icons of grief.

Naruse was well known and respected in Japan for his adaptations of literary works, but I think it is equally important to recognize his depiction of the city. With a few exceptions during the war years, he stuck to *gendai-geki* contemporary settings. Although he often remained in-studio, he crafted an image of Tokyo that seemed unchanged by the war — a city of close-knit neighbors, where commerce and living spaces fluidly overlapped. He did in fact shoot one of the most vivid location-based films of the immediate postwar period, using the devastated Tokyo landscape as the backdrop for a curious political drama in *A Descendant of Taro Urashima* (1946). During the years of the American Occupation, his films featured professional women working as doctors, journalists, teachers and even activists. Over the course of Naruse's career, one can see the changes in the urban landscape and the life of the culture, especially as women's lives were affected.

The following analysis features four of Naruse's films that are currently available on DVD. Both *Meshi* and *Sound of the Mountain* are available from Eureka/Masters of Cinema in the United Kingdom. *Floating Clouds* has been released more recently by BFI in the United Kingdom. For this chapter I have reprinted excerpts from my book on Naruse, based in part on original research exploring the production and critical reception of Naruse's films in Japan. Articles and reviews from newspapers and magazines offer a valuable glimpse into the studio setting and critical context of Japanese cinema during the middle decades of the twentieth century. Even if it looks and feels like art cinema, due to its openness and sensuous aesthetics, superior acting and realist aesthetics, Naruse's cinema was very much anchored in the mass culture of its time. In fact, it was arguably a key component in the way that classical Japanese cinema addressed both men and women.

## *MESHI*: THE SALARYMAN'S WIFE

*Meshi* (*Repast*) opens with an epigraph attributed directly to the author of the original novel, Fumiko Hayashi: "How could I love the pitiful human lives more than I do, the pitiful human lives, which survive in this infinitely wide universe?" The film version of *Meshi* was made in the same year that Hayashi died, 1951, and was based on a serialized story that she left incomplete. Often translated simply as "food," *meshi* also refers to "cooked rice" and to the simple tastes of ordinary people. It also has implications of a useless life, or the unglamorous necessities of life.[1] In adapting Hayashi's novel, Naruse uses the device of voice-over, through which the literary voice of first-person narration so crucial to the modern Japanese novel is used to develop an "interiority" and sense of self.

Hayashi's story was about a marriage, but Naruse's film places the emphasis more directly on the housewife, Michiyo, played by Setsuko Hara. In voice-over she describes her neighborhood in Osaka where the film is set, and then continues to describe her life there over the film's opening shots: "My husband is sitting at the dining table. I go to the kitchen to cook the miso soup. Yesterdays and tomorrows, 365 days a year, we have the same mornings and nights. I wonder if the lives of women are simply to get older and will end in the kitchen and the table." The tedium of everyday life is broken by the arrival of her husband's niece, Satoko (Yukiko Shimazaki), who has run away from her home in Tokyo. Her flirtation with Michiyo's husband, Hatsunosuke (Ken Uehara), disturbs the household, and Michiyo decides to visit her own family in Tokyo to think things over. She meets an old boyfriend, Kazuo (Kan Nihonyanagi), but then learns that Satoko is also interested in him and has even gone to a hot-springs resort with him. Michiyo meets up with her husband in Tokyo and she decides to return to Osaka with him. On the train going back, she says in voice-over: "My husband is sitting beside me. His eyes are closed. His usual profile. A man who is floating in the river called life, he is tired, still fighting. Living with this man, I am seeking happiness for us together. Could it be my true happiness? Maybe this is what a woman's happiness is."

This ambivalent return to the role of housewife is not in Hayashi's original. She left the novel unfinished, just as the husband and wife were establishing their lives apart. At the end of the film, Michiyo may be ready to resign herself to her role as a good wife, but there is nothing in the film to suggest that this

**Fig. 41** Setsuko Hara and Ken Uehara in *Meshi* (Naruse, 1951).

might bring happiness. The contradictions of the ending of *Meshi* are very much in keeping with Hollywood melodrama, in which, as Laura Mulvey has pointed out, more is stirred up than can possibly be settled.[2] Michiyo's decision to return to her humdrum life is motivated only by the lack of options available to her. According to Toshiro Ide, who co-wrote the screenplay with Sumie Tanaka, he and Tanaka thought the film should end with a divorce, but Toho insisted a film that was sympathetic to the wife could not possibly end in divorce. Ide says that, rather than fight for her version, Tanaka walked away from the project.[3] In any case, as one of the contemporary critics, Takao Toda notes, the final voice-over narration does not sound much like Hayashi and he suggests it was added for "mass appeal."[4]

*Meshi* works principally because of the intensity of Michiyo's inchoate desires. She herself seems uncertain of what she wants, and Hara's performance is central to the film's ambivalence and contradictoriness. Although she is attracted to Kazuo, she reminds him that she is still married and is unable to act on her desires. Satoko, the upstart niece, acts on all her impulses and, while she may be depicted as unvirtuous and unwise, there is no question that it is her influence that is deeply unsettling to the marriage. Michiyo is very critical of this modern young woman and yet Satoko's presence enables her to question her life as a housewife. Uehara Ken plays the husband Hatsunosuke as the epitome of the lazy, bored salaryman. The tedium of housework is matched only by the lack of passion in their marriage.

Like the Hollywood melodrama, in *Meshi* there are strong undercurrents of sexuality, of repressions and unspeakable desires that underscore the narrative. And there are also brief explosions of music, bad weather and hysterical laughter that point to these tensions. As Mulvey suggests of Douglas Sirk's women's films, "it is as though the fact of having a female point of view dominating the narrative produces an excess which precludes satisfaction."[5] Despite Hayashi's epigraph that opens the film, it is clear that we are not, after all, being asked simply to pity "*human* lives in this infinitely wide universe," but specifically women's lives in postwar Japan. From Hayashi, Naruse takes the settings of the Osaka and Tokyo neighborhoods and downtown streets. It may be a film about housework but Michiyo's unsettledness is not unrelated to her adventures outside the house.

One critic compares *Meshi* with Ozu's *Early Summer* (*Bakushu*, 1951), pointing out that where "Ozu's world is closed, the world depicted in *Meshi* is an open one." Juzaburo Futaba describes *Meshi* as "a much broader and social work." As a drama of manners (*fuzokugeki*), he says the film is lively and he admires Naruse's ability to sustain the emotional tension. The comparison with *Early Summer* is significant here, as it indicates how the directors' styles were significantly diverging in the postwar era. For Futaba, Naruse's film is more directly connected to contemporary life, whereas he sees Ozu as being preoccupied with the feelings of the older generation in *Early Summer*. *Meshi*, he says, is "not an old curio sitting on a shelf"; indeed, Naruse's narrative is far more grounded in the actions and motivations of the characters, whereas by 1951, Ozu had settled into the stately rhythms of static compositions that mark his mature period.[6]

The Osaka neighborhood where Michiyo and Hatsunosuke live is an extraordinarily detailed set, including a narrow street leading onto a cross street. Many of the neighbors are introduced as secondary characters, providing a flavor that led critic Chiyota Shimizu to say that "the Osaka white-collar worker is shown with a documentary precision and flavour."[7] Michiyo's family house in a Tokyo suburb near Yano Station is likewise handled with care. When Hatsunosuke takes his niece sightseeing through Osaka, leaving Michiyo at home scrubbing floors, the cross-cutting establishes a discrepancy of space and mobility that threatens the marriage. Michiyo's day with her old school friends and her walks through Tokyo are, however, important scenes that place her in public spaces.

Outside the home there is nothing for Michiyo except women envying her marriage and yet, by taking us through these spaces, Naruse situates his story in the historically specific setting of the postwar city. The final reconciliation of the couple is essentially a *deus ex machina*, one that is very reminiscent of Rossellini's *Voyage to Italy* in which George Sanders and Ingrid Bergman, on the verge of a divorce, are miraculously reunited by being swept into a saint's day parade in southern Italy. Michiyo and Hatsunosuke are, likewise, briefly swamped by a crowd of street musicians in Tokyo, and it may be the spirit of the city by which they are able to redeem their lives in Osaka, but it lacks the miraculousness of Rossellini. The contradictions and pitifulness of the lives depicted in *Meshi* are not so easily redeemed, as they are far too embedded in the fabric of postwar Japanese society.

One might argue that Naruse's adaptation of Hayashi transforms her work into melodrama, simply by virtue of the structures of cinematic language and its privileging of the facial close-up. Hara's acting is singled out by many of the contemporary critics and it is, indeed, one of her most nuanced performances. When Michiyo learns that Satoko has not only been flirting with her husband but also has gone out with a man who Michiyo herself has become attracted to since learning of her husband's disloyalties, she says nothing to the girl. Instead she turns away and, sitting on the step to the garden, breaks out into laughter. Fade out to a new scene. Hara relies on gesture and facial expressions to convey her disappointment with her husband and her inarticulate desire for some kind of change in her life, and her performance here goes well beyond the mask-like smile that she is most known for in her films with Ozu.

As a melodramatist, Naruse does not aestheticize suffering in the ways that a director like Mizoguchi does, but remains grounded in the familiar setting of the lower-middle-class home and the *shitamachi*. Inserted close-ups of objects pictured from a high angle that flatten them against the *tatami* floor — an ashtray, coffee cups, shoes — help to establish the detail of material culture that constitute the rituals of everyday life. An ashtray out of place tells a story; shoes turned the wrong way around tell another. A neighbor runs after her husband every morning with the lunch that he repeatedly forgets.

In adapting Hayashi's literature to the screen, there is no question that Naruse was responsible for taming it for public consumption. As Takao Toda noted in a review that carefully compares the film with Hayashi's unfinished novel, Naruse's Osaka is a picture-postcard view of the city, and the film for

**Fig. 42** Yukiko Shimazaki and Setsuko Hara in *Meshi* (Naruse, 1951).

this critic is "the polar opposite of the semi-documentary form which Hayashi Fumiko was trying to work out in her novel."[8] Where she left her characters to wander through the novel without any obvious direction, Naruse's film jettisons the realism of incompletion with the structure of closure. As we shall see in subsequent adaptations, he smoothes out Hayashi's rough edges; but even so, he brought her work to a wider audience and, with actors like Setsuko Hara, brought her characters to life.

From her earliest autobiographical, confessional pieces published in some of the first women's literary journals in the 1920s to her recognition as a novelist in the 1950s, Hayashi's writing was consistently stigmatized by the diminutive label of women's writing. The conundrum of women's writing is, as Ericson notes, only resolved by finding a means of preserving the specificity of female experience without reducing the work to the gendered identity of the author,[9] which suggests the importance of Naruse's contribution. His interest in women's writing and a woman's genre seems to come not from an interest in women or feminism but from the emotionalism and narrative possibilities that he brings out in Hayashi's work.

If several critics accuse him of catering to a mass audience, we need to ask what the gender of that mass audience might be, and to recognize Naruse's accomplishment in bringing this work into the public sphere. *Meshi* was originally scheduled to be directed by Yasuki Chiba, and was offered to Naruse only when Chiba became ill. Toshiro Ide says that it was unusual for Naruse to be asked to substitute for a younger and less established director; moreover, because he had not made a successful film since the 1930s, some Toho executives were reluctant to give him such valuable star-studded property to direct.[10] Ever the company man, Naruse humbly accepted the project, and its huge success propelled him into the next decade with a string of critical and commercial hits.

## SOUND OF THE MOUNTAIN: NARUSE AS MODERNIST

In *Sound of the Mountain* (*Yama no oto*) Naruse replicates the subtlety of his marriage films, casting Setsuko Hara and Ken Uehara as the central child-less couple, but this time the story is adapted from a novel by the Nobel Prize–winning author Yasunari Kawabata. The story of a marriage takes on existential dimensions in Kawabata's narrative. The dramatic intensities of a failing marriage are intersected by the desires and anxieties of the film's protagonist, Shingo (So Yamamura), the father of Uehara's character, Shuichi. Shingo's relationship with his daughter-in-law Kikuko (Hara) is one of deep affection and sympathy, and the more Shuichi screws up the marriage, the closer Shingo and Kikuko become. In a film in which husband and wife never meet each other's gazes, the exchanges of looks between father and daughter-in-law signify a level of understanding and completion that is the film's most striking feature. In true melodramatic fashion, theirs is a doomed relationship, and yet the tenderness and affection between the older man and the younger woman is one of the most passionate relationships in Naruse's oeuvre.

Given Kikuko's status in the household (she calls Shingo "Father"), *Sound of the Mountain* flirts precariously with incest, a theme that is persistent in Japanese literature, and in the New Wave cinema of the 1960s. Moving back and forth between the family home in Kamakura and various locations in Tokyo, the film maps the troubled relationships onto the postwar context. Space, freedom and female subjectivity are the terms with which a melodrama of profound suffering becomes a modernist treatment of postwar Japanese society. The family this time are upper middle class, and their home is a beautiful, sprawling traditional-style building surrounded by a carefully maintained garden. Shingo is something of an aesthete, and the home in Kamakura is virtually cut off from the outside world. Shuichi and Shingo take the train back and forth to work every day, but Kikuko is kept in Kamakura like a hothouse flower.

**Fig. 43** Setsuko Hara in *Sound of the Mountain* (Naruse, 1954).

Although Mizuki Yoko's script is faithful to the Kawabata novel in many respects, she and Naruse once again shift the emphasis from the male perspective to that of a woman's film. The film's poster features Setsuko Hara most prominently, followed by Uehara, with Yamamura reduced to a much smaller figure, suggesting that the studio wanted to capitalize on the success of *Meshi*, produced just 2 years previously. The script also necessarily eliminates a great deal of Shingo's interior monologue, including his ongoing commentary on the physical attributes of the women in his life. Kawabata's protagonist is a man of the old world, and his sexist worldview may be accounted for as a character trait, and yet the novel offers little insight into the minds of any of the other characters. Shingo has a series of erotic dreams that are obliquely linked to the women in his life, and to the deaths of his friends, who die throughout the novel from various causes. In the novel, the old man's mortality underscores all the relationships and the novel's overall worldview.[11] Naruse's version of the story may eliminate the eroticism of Kawabata's prose, but it enables a much fuller depiction of the female characters, especially Kikuko, as desiring subjects.

The family has recently lost their maid, so Kikuko is burdened with an endless series of household chores, which she performs cheerfully despite the fact that her husband sometimes doesn't come home at night, and when he does, he is dead drunk. The critic Kiyo Mikawa noted that female audiences would be bound to sympathize with this depiction of the role of a daughter-in-law — although she also accuses the Kikuko character of being too weak.[12]

Indeed, Kikuko is extraordinarily passive, in keeping with the typical Kawabata heroine — although in the last scene of the film Naruse suggests that there is potential for change. Another critic, Jun Takami, offers a somewhat different perspective, saying that he liked the fact that Shingo's point of view is privileged, but younger audiences might be more interested in the younger characters who he could not appreciate.[13] These critics indicate how this very "literary" film was apprehended in terms of contemporary social issues, no doubt because of Naruse's continued emphasis on the everyday rituals of domestic life.

The final scene of *Sound of the Mountain* has been discussed by several critics as a remarkable commentary on cinematic space. Kikuko calls Shingo at his office and asks to meet him in Shinjuku Garden. She has been away for a few days visiting her own family. As they walk through the huge downtown park she says she has decided to break up with Shuichi. Shingo tells her that Kinu, Shuichi's mistress, is having a child. He also tells her that she should take her freedom for the sake of her own happiness, and they agree to a parting. After reluctantly accepting the freedom that has been granted her, Kikuko looks out at the expanse of meadow and says, "a great deal of attention has been paid to the vista . . . you are able to see to great depths." Shingo asks what a "vista" is, and she answers, "It means the line of an outlook."

Combining elements of French and English garden styles with traditional Japanese, Shinjuku Garden (or Gyoen) was a novelty of Meiji Japan. It opened in 1906 as an imperial garden, and was largely destroyed during the war, reopening

**Fig. 44** So Yamamura and Setsuko Hara in *Sound of the Mountain* (Naruse, 1954).

in 1949 as a national garden open to the public. Shingo and Kikuko walk along tree-lined paths, pausing on a bench with a view of a meadow modeled on an English landscape, designed around a perspectival view. After Kikuko's comment on the vista, Naruse does not follow with her point-of-view shot as might be anticipated but, instead, rests on Hara's close-up as she dabs the tears from her eyes with a faint smile. Shingo looks back at her and then turns to walk away from the camera. She walks into the shot to join him and the film ends with the two figures walking into the distance framed by a large tree in the foreground. Naruse and cameraman Masao Tamai shoot the Shinjuku Garden vista with the same lens that they use in Kamakura, flattening the landscape and focusing on characters in the middle distance and the tree in the foreground. "Nature" in *Sound of the Mountain* exists primarily in the characters' ongoing commentary on seasonal changes and rare species of flowers. On a few occasions shots of the rooftops and distant hills surrounding the Kamakura home are inserted, but they are little more than stock shots. Kikuko and Shingo walk along a receding avenue of leafless trees before reaching the open field in Shinjuku Garden, but the final "vista" is dominated by the foreground tree framing the view, effectively inverting the depth of field.

Naruse and Mizuki have altered Kawabata's original story by taking the lines about the vista away from Shingo and giving them to Kikuko. Significantly, it is the first time that she says something that is not a response to someone else, or the expression of an emotion. To this extent it suggests that she has finally emerged from her suffocating role as daughter-in-law, and the complex feelings she holds for her father-in-law will be resolved into a new perspective on life. Furthermore, this is not the last scene in the novel, but occurs about three-quarters of the way through the book, at the end of which the family has been reunited, Shuichi has left his mistress and they all plan an outing together to the old family home. In Naruse's version, with the Shinjuku Garden scene closing the film, it is far more likely that Kikuko will make a clean break with the family she has married into. As the narrative conclusion, the scene becomes emblematic and suggestive with its implicit reference to cinematic space.

The Japanese critic Shigehiko Hasumi links the Shinjuku Garden scene to several other scenes in Naruse films in which a man and a woman walk together through trees, leaves and shadows. The camera moves with the characters, cutting between them as they converse and within this large spatial expanse the only "orientation" is precisely the relationship itself. Given the absence of fixed points of reference, the man and the woman are virtually alone, despite the intercut shots of other couples and families in the park. For Hasumi, "Yamamura So and Hara Setsuko, as they walk side by side, thus seem to slowly step into endless expansion as the movie meets the movie in its true sense."[14] This reading of the scene recognizes the lack of perspective in the *mise en scène* and links it to the romantic aesthetic with which Naruse has replaced Kawabata's eroticism.

Naruse's romanticism, however ambivalent, embraces the public space available to couples in the newly "democratized" status of Shinjuku Garden that, before the war, had been an imperial garden closed to the public. Shingo notes that it is amazing that "such a park could exist in the middle of Tokyo." Given the love of nature that has been one of the primary bonds between him and his daughter-in-law, the garden envelops them in a utopian discourse of the possible. In the novel, Shingo wonders "did the scene tell one that the youth of the land had been liberated?" While Naruse's script omits these words, I would argue that the sense of possibility is nevertheless registered in the location itself, and in Hara's final smile.

As usual, it is an ambivalent ending, and not only because Naruse's style remains tied to a very different aesthetic than that implied by the reference to perspective and depth. Kikuko is a character drawn to the old ways, and her affection for Shingo is bound up with the wifely duties that she performs for him — bringing him tea, picking up his clothes, and so forth — but she is also of the postwar generation. She has an abortion on her own initiative, telling the family about it only afterwards. Moreover, Naruse's style remains one of observation. Hara's performance of misery, especially after she has had the abortion and cries uncontrollably at home with Shingo and his wife, is extremely powerful, but she is very guarded, much like her persona in Ozu's films of the same period. Kikuko's troubles are highlighted and amplified by Hara's performance, but she never fully escapes the circumscribed roles of wife and daughter-in-law. As a *shoshimin-eiga* and a woman's film, the existential dilemma is not that of Shingo's mortality, but Kikuko's freedom.

The other women in the film are far more outspoken and articulate their troubles much more directly than does Kikuko. Shuichi's sister Fusako (Chieko Nakakita) is a single mother with two children. She accuses her father of having married her to an unreliable mate who has left her, and she points out how much kinder he is to his daughter-in-law than to her. Kinu, Shuichi's mistress (Reiko Sumi), is a war widow with her own dressmaking business. She believes that she deserves to have another woman's husband as her lover, and to have his child, because of her loss. She can do without Shuichi, who she says beats her violently. A fourth young woman, Eiko (Yoko Sugi), frequents dance halls with both Shingo and Shuichi, but eventually takes Shingo to Kinu's home out of sympathy for Kikuko. Together with Kinu's roommate Ikeda (Yatsuko Tanami), the film features four young single women, all trying to make their way in a world in which men like Shuichi have been psychologically destroyed by the war.

From Kawabata, Naruse has developed an aesthetic vocabulary with which to explore the contradictions of Japanese modernity. The simplicity and harmony of the garden, the *Noh* mask that Shingo acquires from a deceased friend, the architecture of the house — all these things can't stop the dissolution of Shingo's family. His affection for Kikuko is a blind against the failed marriages of his children and a foil for his own mortality. And yet Naruse also counters the individualism of Kawabata's novel by placing Shingo within a constellation of characters, whose relationships are articulated through composition and framing, in keeping with the conventions of the *shoshimin-eiga*. Within the terms of the observational style of the *shoshimin-eiga*, the aesthetics of the old world are incompatible with love, romance and the desire to escape from restrictive social roles. Shuichi himself, while on one level a despondent salaryman, seems driven to adultery by the stasis and formality of his father's home.

Hara's performance, in which gesture, facial expression and glances say far more than her words, has a mask-like aura. The mask for Hara constitutes a kind of doubleness, as if her "well-proportioned beauty" were only one layer, the public one, of a more complex personality that remains hidden beneath it. By 1954 Hara had acquired the iconic power of Japan's "eternal virgin," having starred in a long series of war films, followed by Kurosawa's "democracy" picture *No Regrets for our Youth* (*Waga seishun ni kuinashi*, 1946), and a string of Ozu *shoshimin-eiga*, including *Late Spring* (*Banshun*, 1949), *Early Summer* (*Bakushu*) and *Tokyo Story* (*Tokyo monogatari*, 1953). Her star image was thus closely bound to the national imaginary, in which the ideology of the virgin harbored an ideal of cultural purity. Setsuko Hara's screen persona is one of tight control under which a current of strong emotion can often be detected. Part of her popular appeal was due to a certain honesty and integrity of character, enhanced by the *shoshimin-eiga* genre that kept her in extremely plain costumes. However, she also excelled in expressing highly contradictory and conflicted emotions. She can be at once hopeful and doubtful at marriage proposals; she laughs when she is most sad and cries when she is most happy. The contradictions and tensions within Hara's star image are very much bound up with a nativist sensibility, a longing for the past combined with a recognition of the impossibility of such a return. Among her secrets is her reputed quarter-German heritage that may account for her slightly Caucasian look.

Hara's sexuality is in the end her biggest secret: she retired after her last film with Ozu, to live alone in Kamakura. According to Donald Richie, her disappearance at age 43 was the cause of great resentment, especially as she has remained a recluse ever since, closely protecting her privacy. She refused to grow old in public. The spectacle of the woman's body may have been a key ingredient of Japanese modernity, but it also tended to repress the emergence of female subjectivity. In the 1950s the construction of femininity remained precariously balanced between subjectivity and a protection of traditional gender roles, and Hara Setsuko arguably played a crucial role in the display of this balance. Through her performance, and the changes made to Kawabata's story, *Sound of the Mountain* most eloquently details the difficulties of female emancipation and the contradictions of female subjectivity within Japanese modernity. The price of freedom for Kikuko is the loss of her father-in-law and the aesthetics of nature, simplicity and the old world with which he is identified.

## *FLOATING CLOUDS*: NARRATIVE AND MEMORY

*Floating Clouds* (*Ukigumo*) is a film with an epic span. Due to its engagement with the geopolitical history of the immediate postwar period, it has found a special place in the national imagination, and tends to be Naruse's best-known film in Japan. As Freda Freiberg notes, its popularity may be in part due to the popularity of Hayashi Fumiko's best-selling novel.[15] In the opening shots of the film, Hideko Takamine as Yukiko emerges from a series of stock shots of repatriated Japanese civilians trudging home after the war. Because Yukiko's story includes flashbacks to her wartime posting in Indochina and her liaison with an American GI in Tokyo, it intersects with controversial social issues that by 1955 were rapidly becoming a history at risk of being forgotten. The story of *Floating Clouds* is focused on a love affair between Yukiko and another repatriated civilian, but their romance cannot be disentangled from the postwar conditions that the lovers confront on their return to Japan, and the trajectory of their affair is an expression of the state of the defeated nation as a society adrift. Based on Hayashi's last completed novel (1949–51), the title *Ukigumo* (which is frequently translated as "Drifting Clouds") is a common metaphor for an aimless life. Hayashi borrowed the title from Shimei Futabatei's "first modern novel" (1887–89), shifting the emphasis from the male to the female protagonist.[16]

Takamine's character Yukiko is a typically stubborn and resilient Hayashi heroine, although not without a sense of humor when she witnesses her relative (and occasional lover) Iba perpetuate a fraudulent religious cult for profit (she eventually manages to steal most of his proceeds from him). Her lover Tomioka (Masayuki Mori), although largely unemployed, is in some respects similar to the salarymen in Naruse's marriage films: a despondent and irresponsible man, prone to drinking and womanizing and not in control of his own life, shuffled around the country by the powers that be. He is very much the embodiment of the defeated nation, while Yukiko's attachment to him is filtered through a series of social roles that she assumes — from prostitute to religious cult manager — in order to survive. Paul Willemen and Freda Freiberg offer interpretive commentaries on the film on the BFI release, debating the unusually masochistic character of Yukiko, but both conclude that she is in fact the stronger of the two "out-of-synch" lovers.

Despite the familiarity of these characters, *Floating Clouds* is an anomalous film and represents a significant departure for Naruse. It was not the first time he had used stock shots or flashbacks, but they participate here in a complex narrative structure in which memory and time become much more prominent features than in the spatialized narratives — the *shoshimin-eiga* — with which he had become identified. In the absence of Naruse's favored domestic set of the *shoshimin-eiga* the characters and the film lack stability,[17] but an unusual sense of instability is created. The couple pass through one or two homes, but they never stay. They are constantly on the move, through Tokyo, to a hot-springs resort (Ikaho) and finally to Kagoshima and the island of Yakushima in Kyushu in southern Japan. They meet in inns and bars, they stroll together through the ruined streets of the city, through parks and through the forests of Indochina. Yukiko lives briefly in a small "storage house" as the companion of an American GI (who is merely glimpsed and overheard in passing), and briefly as Iba's mistress in an elegant, well-appointed home; Tomioka lives in a suburban home until he sells it and sends his wife to the countryside. He rents a room in a tenement surrounded by children playing in the corridors.

Despite their repeated attempts to rekindle the love they experienced in Dalat during the war, Yukiko and Tomioka cannot find happiness in postwar Japan. She is especially persistent in seeking him out, but he is ambivalent, unwilling to commit to her, until the final scenes in which she accompanies him to Yakushima, contracts tuberculosis and dies alone in the mountains in a thunderstorm. Only as she becomes ill and finally dies does Tomioka display any real affection for Yukiko. Until that point, he seems drawn to her almost helplessly, but at the same time drawn to other women as well. Because of his womanizing, Yukiko becomes the sympathetic focal point of the narrative. It is her story and her death to which the meandering narrative finally leads.

**Fig. 45** Hideko Takamine in *Floating Clouds* (Naruse, 1955).

Hayashi's original narration actually shifts between the two protagonists' inner thoughts,[18] whereas in the film Yukiko's perspective is unambiguously privileged. While she suffers, Tomioka is cold-hearted, apparently taking advantage of her affections. Jean Douchet points out that as a "ladies man," Tomioka "likes his ladies dead."[19] Indeed, Yukiko's death is preceded by those of

Tomioka's wife (of natural causes) and a woman named Osei (Mariko Okada) with whom he had an affair while visiting Ikaho with Yukiko (Osei is killed by her husband, possibly out of jealousy). Douchet's ironic comment points to the way that, while Yukiko is hopelessly stuck on one man, Tomioka moves carelessly through a series of women. Yukiko's last words to her lover accuse him of being a womanizer, causing her undue stress in her weakened condition. Indeed, the novel ends with Tomioka leaving Yakushima to meet up with a woman he met on the way there.[20] *Floating Clouds* is very much a love story, with all the pathos and melodrama that the genre entails.

Mitsuhiro Yoshimoto has offered a provocative reading of *Floating Clouds* in terms of national allegory. In his view, the suffering of the couple "is in some sense a form of punishment for their complicit relationship with Japanese imperialism." He explains as follows:

> The ultimate death of the woman in Yakushima, which resembles the jungle of Southeast Asia, seems to confirm this reading of the film. Naruse's seemingly apolitical melodrama is in fact one of the most subtle yet severe indictments of Japanese imperialism and of the responsibilities of ordinary people who benefited from Japanese colonial enterprise.[21]

For Yoshimoto, the film stands out for its refusal to follow through on the "conversion narrative" of postwar Japanese melodrama in which prewar Japan is "converted" seamlessly into the new postwar society, a conversion that depends on the denial of the war and its emergence from prewar modernity. In his reading of *Floating Clouds*, the Takamine character "refuses to convert . . . to a comfortable ordinary life in postwar Japan," and the film demonstrates that "Japan as an imagined community is often reconstructed only at the expense of women."[22]

While Yoshimoto's interpretation accounts for the woman's sacrifice and points to the ways that *Floating Clouds* departs from contemporary narrative treatments of the war, the characters cannot be said to feel responsible for their role in the war. On the contrary, the flashbacks of Dalat constitute a dreamlike fantasy. Tomioka served as an official in the Imperial Forestry Ministry, and Yukiko was posted there as a typist, but the imagery is more that of a country retreat than a workplace. They meet in an elegant colonial mansion where they are served by local servants (one of whom Tomioka flirts with) and they stroll together through a pastoral landscape of babbling brooks, leafy forests and flowery meadows. Dalat is a virtual escape from Japanese social conventions, an escape that they hope to recapitulate in their journey to Yakushima, where Tomioka finally finds a new posting. The final flashback, inserted as Tomioka weeps over the body of Yukiko, features Takamine dressed in white, skipping (in white platform shoes) down a forest path in Dalat.

As Susanna Fessler notes of Hayashi's novel, "there is an overall sense of loss: loss of innocence, loss of love, and loss of experience."[23] Hayashi herself traveled through China and Southeast Asia during the war, writing reports from the front that were nothing if not consistent with official propaganda. Her failure to apologize for these activities was criticized after the war,[24] and there is little evidence that *Floating Clouds* constituted any kind of remorse on her part. I would argue that, contrary to Yoshimoto's interpretation, the deep ambivalence of both novel and film lies in the implicit memory of wartime as a kind of utopian paradise.

**Fig. 46** Masayuki Mori and Hideko Takamine in *Floating Clouds* (Naruse, 1955).

The romantic memory of Dalat propels the film to its final tragic conclusion. The destiny of the lovers is precisely the failure to recover their experience as colonial expatriates. When they finally arrive in Yakushima in a torrential downpour, Yukiko needs to be carried on a stretcher from the boat. In some respects this is Takamine's most glamorous role in a Naruse film, and she is frequently lit with a soft light in which she positively glows, with her hair loose and, in a number of instances, dressed in the flashy outfits of a mistress or prostitute. Her death scene, in which she crawls across the floor to close a banging shutter, coughing and crying all the way, is high melodrama. The woman nursing her enters the house, and Tomioka, far away in a hill station, suddenly turns to the camera intuitively sensing Yukiko's death (an image that would be recapitulated by Nagisa Oshima in *Cruel Story of Youth* in 1960). Several times they have contemplated double suicide, using it as an excuse to travel to remote inns, where they inevitably call it off due to lack of will or inspiration and some obscure desire to live.

By the time they go to Yakushima, Tomioka has finally found a job and Yukiko has successfully stolen ¥300,000 from Iba, who took advantage of her before the war. In the inn in Kagoshima, where the lovers wait to travel to the island, the staff refer to Yukiko as "madam," and they are finally recognized as husband and wife. But, in true melodramatic fashion, it is too late. Yukiko has already fallen ill and their happiness will forever elude them. As Douchet notes, this is a film with no future, a film in which people are doomed to live in a perpetual present tense, "a time of love, not a time of desire."[25] Perhaps this is a kind of punishment; perhaps their desire is too closely tied to an experience deemed in the postwar period to be invalid and unacceptable to be reawakened after the war. Yukiko may be a thief, but that is her only crime. She went to Dalat to escape the dismal domestic situation that she endured with her sister's family and in-laws. The war offered her an opportunity to escape the Japanese institutions of womanhood, even if it turned out to be a false hope. Yukiko and Tomioka are not characters who have committed a crime; they are characters caught up in the sweep of history over which they have no control, as the *deus ex machina* of Yukiko's death insists.

The sense of a perpetual present tense, cut off from future and past, is precisely the achievement of Naruse's film, which once again transposes a melodramatic woman's film into a modernist idiom. The narrative transitions from one space to another, moving abruptly from hovel to mansion, to family home, to black market storage shed, from public park to hot-springs resort, are always abrupt. Indefinite amounts of time pass between sequences and the transitions are rarely established or prepared for. In one 2-minute scene demonstrating

Naruse's narrative economy, Yukiko has an abortion and reads of Osei's death in the hospital. In many much longer scenes, Yukiko and Tomioka sit by a table in a sparsely furnished inn or restaurant, drinking, smoking, recounting their last parting or planning their next ill-fated encounter. At one point they pass a crowd of striking workers singing "The Internationale" (in another scene that Oshima would revisit in the opening scenes of *Cruel Story of Youth*). The lovers are sidelined by history, on the margins of postwar society.

**Fig. 47** Masayuki Mori and Hideko Takamine in *Floating Clouds* (Naruse, 1955).

In her obsessive passion for Tomioka, Yukiko comes to resemble a heroine like those of nineteenth-century Victorian literature, focusing her entire being on a man who is clearly undeserving of her affections. For his part, Tomioka is a romantic hero: charming and rugged, associated with the outdoors, a man whom women seem to continually throw themselves at. Yukiko is forced into other liaisons for the sake of survival, and stoops even to thievery to seduce Tomioka (she calls him to join her after she robs Iba), and yet she is wholly defined by a single-minded passion. The excessiveness of her relentless pursuit of Tomioka may be seen as an expression of female desire that cannot be contained by a repressive society. Postwar Japan, like Victorian England, offered women education but little opportunity for career advancement or professional status. Yukiko's skills as a typist and an accountant are not enough for her to support herself, and so she is compelled to use her body for profit.

Through the late 1950s and 1960s, as Takamine played more romantic roles, Naruse's cinema would more and more resemble the tragic fatalism of Victorian literature in which women's suffering is expressed in endlessly frustrated romantic relationships.

The mobility and meandering narrative of *Floating Clouds* follows the two protagonists through a series of iconic locations, including ruined sections of Tokyo,[26] the forested woodlands of the Izu Peninsula, the wharf in Kagoshima where Mori looks for a boat, the crowded Ikebukuro marketplace and the hot-springs town of Ikaho for which Naruse used a rare crane shot to film the lovers walking up and down the steep, shadowed stairs of the village. The film includes many emblematic shots of the lovers: in the bath, in the rain, on a boat, among the ruins, and so forth. As Hasumi remarks, the image of "a man and a woman" is most powerful in this film, as they alone anchor and connect these disparate public and private spaces.[27] Often their despair is registered only in sorrowful looks and dejected poses, huddled around a brazier to keep warm or walking together through desolate landscapes.

As Douchet notes, the relentless flow of the narration creates the sense of a void. "Life, a constant presence, flows incessantly, simply because this kind of life is unstoppable. But it has no meaning in it, it is empty."[28] He further accounts for Naruse's occasional disruptions of continuity editing in this film as an inversion of space, which "jolts the senses." Indeed, *Floating Clouds* is Naruse's most formally ambitious film in its elliptical narrative structure and deep ambivalence regarding the memory of war. It was a rare film in 1955 that dealt so squarely with the sorrow of a defeated nation, and a reactionary reading in which Yukiko's death is symbolic of a national death is as valid as Yoshimoto's more progressive interpretation of it as an indictment of imperialism.

Noriko Mizuta's assessment of Hayashi's novel is true of the film as well: "Through her depiction of Yuikiko's wandering amid the emptiness and desolation of the defeat that marked the end of modernity in Japan," Hayashi presents "an impossibility of development."[29] The parallels with *Rashomon* may go further than their shared borrowing of Ravel's *Boléro* for their soundtracks. Like Kurosawa's film, *Floating Clouds* conveys a depth of uncertainty and instability, although in this case, due to its setting, it is more intricately linked to postwar Japanese society, and significantly lacks the optimistic finale of *Rashomon*. There is no social rebirth on the horizon at the end of *Floating Clouds*. The paradise that the lovers dream of and remember becomes Yukiko's graveyard, and Tomioka is doomed to drift aimlessly after she dies.

## WHEN A WOMAN ASCENDS THE STAIRS: A WORLD OF APPEARANCES

From his earliest silent films of the 1930s, Mikio Naruse was drawn to the streets of downtown Tokyo. In several films of the 1950s he reconstructed the downtown neighborhoods in studio sets to preserve their prewar cache. In 1960, with *When a Woman Ascends the Stairs*, he returned to the Ginza area of downtown Tokyo, this time complete with the bar signs, neon lights and traffic of the postwar city. The brief passages of location shooting set the mood for the film, although it relies heavily on studio sets, resulting in a unique mix of old-fashioned narrow streets and the cosmopolitan corporate culture of high finance and expensive entertainment in 1960s Tokyo. Keiko (Hideko Takamine) works as a bar hostess in this renovated "floating world," where she struggles to keep her head up and her integrity intact. This is one of Naruse's best-known films outside Japan and it well deserves the attention it has received. Not only is it an emotionally sustained melodrama of unrequited love but also it has a strong documentary flavor, enhanced by Keiko's sporadic voice-over, which offers a commentary on the life of a Ginza bar hostess.

Japanese hostess bars have more or less replaced the geisha business that in postwar Japan became increasingly marginalized as an archaic practice, too expensive for most Japanese and preserved as little more than a tourist attraction. After the war, the *mizu shobai* evolved into a new kind of bar in which women entertain men primarily by pouring drinks and flirting with them. Hostess bars serve the modern business community, their fates rising and falling with the Japanese yen. They still flourish today, featuring exotic arrays of foreign women, and are matched by a new variety of "host bars" serving women clients. The early 1960s was when the industry exploded as a glamorous form of nighttime entertainment, with bars flourishing in the big cities, some of them employing thousands of girls, and other, smaller clubs reserved for an elite clientele.[30]

Shot in black-and-white Tohoscope by Masao Tamai, *When a Woman* is one of Naruse's most formally interesting films of the 1960s. The interiors are almost always framed in medium shot, both for Western-furnished rooms (which

**Fig. 48** *When a Woman Ascends the Stairs* (Naruse, 1960).

predominate) and for Japanese-style rooms. The consistency of the two-shot framing of characters seen from the waist up on left and right sides of the frame is comically announced in an early scene in which two pairs of women gossiping about a bar hostess who has recently committed suicide are matched together. The women may be different but, like their conversation, they are identical in their spatial position in the frame. With this fairly tight framing, all the interior spaces appear cramped and small. Keiko's expensive apartment is tiny, and yet quite a lot of activity takes place around her small dining table, which fills the foreground of most of the shots.

The detail within the *mise en scène* is especially pronounced in this framing, adding to the "documentary" aspect of the film. Foreign audiences who are unfamiliar with this very Japanese institution may assume that Japanese audiences would necessarily know all about them. In fact, the level on which Keiko works is a rarefied world accessible only to salarymen in the upper echelons of corporate culture. Even to Japanese audiences in 1960, and to contemporary audiences, the film provided a rare picture of a glamorous and racy world. Keiko, however, doesn't truly belong in this milieu, as several characters tell her, and the narrative in actual fact turns on the difference of her character. Like Naruse's two previous films about women working in the *mizu shobai,* *Late Chrysanthemums* and *Flowing*, this film bridges the social gap between the domestic world of married women and that of "professional" women, or women working in the *mizu shobai*. As Iijima puts it in his review, the film is about "how the very intelligent and middle-aged widow or the unmarried woman who does not have any specific skills or talents, and is not part of the clerical workforce, makes a living in contemporary society."[31]

Keiko is a widow, whose husband was hit by a truck some time after the war ended. When he died, she vowed never to love another man and, indeed, she harbors a loyalty to the past that is also a sign of her moral integrity and virtue in a debased milieu. Over the course of the film she has no fewer than four suitors, three of whom are identified in an early bar scene. Her fellow hostess Junko (Reiko Dan) points them out to another woman: the richest man, Goda (Ganjiro Nakamura); the banker Fujisaki (Masayuki Mori); and the fat man, Sekine (Daisuke Kato). Sekine doesn't have a chance with Keiko, says Junko, and besides, he's married. Unfortunately, Keiko doesn't know this and falls hard for Sekine when he proposes to her.

In a film that takes place almost all at night, the ups and downs of this particular upset are expressed through sunlight. After Sekine proposes to her, we see Keiko happily cleaning her apartment with sunlight streaming through the windows. The phone rings, and it is Sekine's wife looking for him. Dressed in her fancy *kimono* and cloak, Keiko goes out to the suburbs where she speaks to the wife in an empty lot with smokestacks behind them and children playing noisily around them. The space and the sunlight make a striking contrast to the rest of the film, even if it is a depressing sight. Sekine turns out to be a somewhat disturbed individual who plays at being someone he isn't. His psychosis is endemic to the modern metropolis, and the scene puts Keiko's thwarted desires in the clear light of day. She wasn't in love with him, but fell for the lure of a home and a husband. The bright lighting of the scene underlines the fact that things are not always as they appear in Ginza.

The modernity of *When a Woman* lies in its treatment of the world of appearances that is the Ginza. In this respect, the film might be compared with Douglas Sirk's 1959 film *Imitation of Life*. Bypassing the Manichean dualisms of the American film, Naruse's melodrama locates its tensions within a single character who struggles to remain true to herself within the deceptions and con-tradictions of her world. An ongoing commentary on fashion and the expenses that a woman like Keiko needs to incur includes the costs of *kimono*, luxury apartments and taxis. She often ends her day, slightly drunk, at home with her abacus, calculating the day's receipts. But despite all the time and money she spends on her appearance, Keiko is criticized by a bar proprietress for dressing too conservatively, and by her mother who criticizes her for being too flashy. While most of her colleagues at the hostess bars wear dresses — usually with sparkles or frills and plunging necklines — Keiko sticks to *kimono* and is never seen dressed otherwise. Less a sign of "tradition" than of class, Keiko always looks more dignified than the other girls; indeed, her *kimono* are likely to be far more expensive than their ready-to-wear fashions. At the hairdresser, she tries to avoid a style that might make her appear "too matronly," as she is somewhat older than the other hostesses.

**Fig. 49** Reiko Dan and Hideko Takamine in *When a Woman Ascends the Stairs* (Naruse, 1960).

Keiko is, in fact, a *mama-san*, which means that she is the head hostess in a bar, responsible for cultivating personal relationships with the customers. Businessmen come with their employees and associates to a given club in order to visit the *mama-san*, who makes sure they are provided with the best service — that is, hostesses to chat and drink with. The men may have their "favorites" among the girls, but the *mama-san* sets the tone and the standard for the club. While she may appear to hold power within her bar, Keiko is, in fact, caught within a complicated hierarchy of management. She does not own the bars she works in, but is responsible for currying favor with the clients, and making sure they pay. When business is bad, all the blame rests with her.

The plot of *When a Woman* interweaves Keiko's love life with her attempts to succeed in the dog-eat-dog world of the *mizu shobai*. Yuri starts her own bar with the supportive patronage of a certain businessman, and, indeed, Keiko receives a similar offer from Mr. Goda (Nakamura) from Osaka. He places a huge stack of cash on the table between them, but she refuses his terms, which include weekends with him when he visits Tokyo. Keiko's young protégée, Junko, is not so proud and is quite happy to have Goda set her up in exchange for a bit of that-which-is-never-named (but is most definitely implied). Keiko's plan for her own bar is to collect "subscriptions" from her wealthy clients, enough to invest in her own establishment. She intends to run the bar with her manager Komatsu (Tatsuya Nakadai) who works for her at the Lilac and at the Carton where she moves shortly after the rebuke from the boss of the Lily. Komatsu may be Keiko's employee, but he keeps an eye on her working the bar, berating her for being rude, on occasion, to clients. Among Komatsu's jobs is the collecting of debts from the patrons who seem to frequent the bars on credit. Keiko's plan to raise money from people who are already in debt to her seems somewhat far-fetched. Nevertheless, it is testimony to her persistence and tenacity, and this is what it takes to climb the stairs day after day.

Keiko's voice-over monologue, sporadic as it is, serves a number of functions in the film, providing narrative information and poetic reflection, often intermingling the two in a subjective commentary. At one point she betrays the fact that business and pleasure cannot be so easily separated. Entering a tall office building, she says, "For women on this street, life is a battle I must not lose." She explains the objective of the subscription book, and then adds, "I hate discussing money with the man I love," and she enters Fujisaki's office. Fujisaki is a married man but, despite her own vow of chastity, she is hopelessly attracted to him. Masayuki Mori, naturally, plays the role of heartthrob exceedingly well. When they finally spend the night together, it comes very close to being romantic. A spilled glass beside the bed is the token signal of a consummated affair but, Fujisaki quickly proves himself to be a cad. Before he leaves her in the morning, he announces that he is being transferred to Osaka and that he hasn't the courage to break up his family by taking a mistress. He leaves her some valuable stocks, sealing her complicity with and dependency on the corporate world. In the final scene of the film, she sees him off at the train station, deeply embarrassing him by returning the stocks directly to his wife — and not forgetting a toy for the child. The wife is impressed, sensing Keiko's sophistication, and comments that she doesn't look like a bar hostess.

Keiko may get the last word in with Fujisaki, but we leave her climbing the stairs once again to the bar, saying "Certain trees bloom no matter how cold the wind." Her monologue from the outset contains references to the changing seasons, in keeping with the poetry of the "floating world." The discourse on appearances may be a modern gesture, but insofar as the film invokes the aesthetics of transience (*mono no aware*) in Keiko's voice-over, it links the glamor of the modern city to a much older discourse of everyday life in Tokyo's pleasure quarters. Keiko's opening lines are indicative of this blending of the old and the new: "On late autumn afternoons, bars near the Ginza are like girls without makeup."

Night in the city in *When a Woman* is very much a display, and the film has numerous shots of the corridor-like streets stacked with lights receding into the distance. The stairs that Keiko repeatedly climbs lead to different bars, but they are always framed the same way — as a chute that seems to suck her up. Close-ups of her *tabi*-adorned feet (*tabi* are white socks that are worn with *kimono* and sandals) are inserted each time, making little visual *haiku* from the film's title. The lighting in these stairwells and in the bars themselves contains multiple discreet sources, creating textured chiaroscuro effects in which the white feet glow briefly. The overall aesthetic of the film is distinctly noirish, even if it is not a film about a crime. The tight framing of interior spaces, along with the ongoing discussion of real estate and rent, make this an emblematic city film, but it is also very much a women's film.

There may be no crime committed, but women are hurt, and their heartbreaks and their suicides are inseparable from the business in which they work. Yuri dies from an accidental suicide that she stages in order to deflect her creditors. Her benefactor — like all the men in Keiko's life — turns out to be a heartless exploiter who tries to collect Yuri's debts from her poor mother. Keiko's final slap in the face comes from her long-time friend and manager Komatsu. When he finds out about her liaison with Fujisaki he hits her and calls her a tramp. He says he has loved her all along, but respected her vow on her husband's grave, and always respected her. It's a rather hysterical moment in the film, with Keiko demanding that he leave before she screams, and Nakadai's extroverted performance style gets briefly out of Naruse's control. And yet, as the penultimate scene, it finally separates all the men from the women whose world they control. Keiko's chances for a fulfilling relationship seem to be as slim as her chances of owning her own bar one day.

The Ginza world is contrasted by the depiction of Keiko's home life. She retreats to recover from an ulcer at her mother's home in Tsukudajima, a waterfront neighborhood not far from Ginza. However, both her mother and her brother bleed her for money. Naruse refrains from his usual framing of

Japanese domestic interiors, perhaps because of the widescreen framing that limits editing choices, so that the home itself is devoid of the familiar aesthetic values of balance and spatial harmony that he often uses for these working-class settings. There is a realist element in Keiko's support of her poor family, but the contrast between the two worlds also feeds into Keiko's ambivalence toward marriage. She has no illusions about domestic life, spending so much of her time with married men, even if she occasionally fantasizes about it as an alternative to her own struggle for survival.

Like his other films set in the milieu of the demimonde, Naruse provides a glimpse into the everyday lives of so-called "professionals," revealing the details and routines of their parallel world. This includes the detail of material culture — kimono, perfumes, beauty parlor paraphernalia and whiskey brands — and Keiko serves a Western breakfast in her apartment complete with toast and a coffee service. The film includes a brief lesson on the role of sex in the hostess bar business, when Keiko says in her voice-over: "Around midnight, Tokyo's 16,000 bar women go home. The best go home by car, second-rate ones by streetcar, and the worst go to inns with their customers." Shots of anonymous women on the night-lit streets illustrate Keiko's words. Keiko would count herself as among "the best," and yet she is not above taking a very special customer home with her. The night with Fujisaki includes a fair amount of drinking, as she is on the rebound from her disastrous liaison with Sekine, and by letting her guard down she reveals, however briefly, that her vow to her dead husband is as much a survival tactic as anything else.

Keiko, like many Narusian heroines before her, is caught within a fixed social system. If she tries hard, she can succeed in this world, but there is in actual fact no way out, except through marriage, should she be lucky enough to find a reliable man. The example of the proprietress who owns the second bar that she works at is evidence that it is possible for women to move to the top in this business. The difficulty facing Keiko is how to satisfy her womanly desires to be loved in a world where no one can be trusted and romance and flirtation is the name of the game.

Far from being critical of the hostess bar scene, When a Woman depicts the epitome of modern, cosmopolitan Tokyo. The English-language bar signs, the foreign-looking and foreign-sounding men and women in the bars (accents and skin colors suggest other Asian ethnicities) and the latest fashions and cars all create a sensuous environment that seduces the viewer as much as it does the rich clients. Key to this sensuous appeal is the soundtrack by Toshiro Mayuzumi, which introduces a soft jazz theme over the opening credits. (Mayuzumi provided scores for most of Imamura's films of the 1960s; this was his only collaboration with Naruse.) Although music is used only sporadically throughout the film, the background sounds of "lounge music" give the film a very contemporary feel. Even 45 years later, the film can still be said to have captured something that persists in the Tokyo nightlife. The cosmopolitan veneer is, however, just another veil over a social institution that is thoroughly Japanese in its regulation of gender roles.

*When a Woman* is also one of Takamine's finest performances. Her character may only be 30 years old, but she is extraordinarily worldly and sophisticated. Takamine exposes her vulnerabilities while always maintaining a certain poise. Her characterization benefits from the contrast with Junko, the young hostess who moves in with her and steals the patron Goda from under her nose. Reiko Dan's performance is bubbly and girlish, just as her clothes are frilly and loud. She is almost like a daughter figure in the film, representing a new generation of women. Keiko is her mentor and friend and forgives her for stealing Goda, but in their world, no one can be trusted. Yuri betrays Keiko early in the film by stealing her customers, but they make up shortly before she dies. This is a woman's world, despite its reliance on men, and Keiko's character is emotionally bonded not only to the other hostesses but also to the various wives on the periphery of her world. *When a Woman* is not simply a beautifully crafted film; it remains one of the only Japanese films to explore a woman's view of the world of Tokyo hostess bars.

*Chapter Six*

# Remembering the War: Three Postwar War Films

uring the 15-year war, or the "Greater East Asian War," as it is sometimes called,[1] a great number of war films illustrated the hardships and
heroic actions of the Japanese military. As the war increased and inten-
sified in the 1940s, more and more filmmaking resources were commandeered
for the war effort. During these difficult years, the film industry was completely
at the service of the military command. Many personnel refused to cooperate;
many more were drafted; and many continued to do the best they could under
the circumstances to maintain their livelihoods. Newsreels depicted action on
the front, troops on parade, and munitions production; many films also featured domestic activities on the home front supporting the war effort. Despite
the diminishing resources, the war really established the full scope and influence of the Japanese cinema as a mode of mass culture. As a tool of imperialist
propaganda — along with radio and newspapers — it inevitably contributed to
the unprecedented sense of invincibility that characterized Japanese wartime
ideology.

With the surprising surrender of Emperor Hirohito in August 1945, following
the devastating blows delivered to Hiroshima and Nagasaki, the propaganda
machine abruptly shifted gears. The American Occupation banned any and all
depictions of military activities, including *jidai-geki* tales of samurai warriors,
and they encouraged filmmakers to include more sexuality and "kissing" to make

their films seem more like American films. The 1945–52 period has been referred to as "the Confusion era," as Japanese cultural producers struggled to adapt to the new "democratic" mandates of the Occupation regime.[2] It wasn't until after the Occupation in 1952 that filmmakers were free to handle the sensitive subject of the wartime experience without recourse to allegorical frameworks such as those Kurosawa used in *Rashomon*. Most Japanese families had lost relatives in the war, and the process of repatriation was long and slow.

Although the war is a backdrop of some kind in almost all Japanese films through the 1950s, there are some key titles in which memories of the war have thoroughly penetrated everyday life. These include *A Japanese Tragedy* (Kinoshita, 1953), *Twenty-Four Eyes* (Kinoshita, 1954) and *Floating Clouds* (Naruse, 1955). While these films feature female protagonists whose lives have been irrevocably altered by the wartime experience, only a few filmmakers during the 1950s returned to the actual battlefields. One of the most salient topics of the postwar war film was the question of repatriation, and many key films, including those discussed here, are set outside Japan in the territories that had been occupied by the imperial army. In the aftermath of the surrender, many men were abandoned without leadership or supplies in vast areas of Southeast Asia and mainland China. Neither war heroes nor innocent victims of the conflict, they enabled an investigation of Japanese identity in the new transnational context of postwar democracy, peace and reconciliation. Moreover, the barren landscapes of war-ravaged Asia provided an ideal setting for the existential questions arising from a war fought with such patriotic fervor and lost with such a crushing blow.

The cinema played a central role in helping the nation accomplish what Mitsuhiro Yoshimoto describes as a "conversion narrative."[3] The 1945 surrender became a kind of ideological pivot point, around which cultural producers had to reinvent a Japanese identity that had some continuity with the past but that would also be consistent with the expectations of a democratic modern nation. Because complicity with wartime activities could not be condoned, most films avoided the topic as much as possible. Thus, the "confusion" of "the Confusion era" settled into a familiar palimpsest of ideological contradiction diffused by melodramatic pathos, aesthetic sensualism and modernist irony and fragmentation. The struggle to remember the war dead was — and continues to be — an unresolved tension in Japanese culture. The three films discussed here, two by

Kon Ichikawa — *The Burmese Harp* and *Fires on the Plain* — and one by Masaki Kobayashi — *The Human Condition* — are exemplary of how this struggle was translated into the cinematic vocabulary of landscape and psychology.

## RETURN TO SOUTHEAST ASIA: TWO WAR FILMS BY ICHIKAWA

Kon Ichikawa's two films about the defeat of the Japanese army in Southeast Asia are among the few Japanese films to tackle the brutal end of the Pacific War directly. In many respects, they are the closest precursors to Clint Eastwood's treatment of the subject in *Letters from Iwo Jima* (2006). The revival of Japanese cinema in the 1950s, often described as postwar humanism, may have been instigated by the humbling history of national defeat, and yet the topic was more often treated obliquely and allegorically, displaced onto more remote historical settings. With *The Burmese Harp* (a.k.a. *Harp of Burma*, 1956) and *Fires on the Plain* (1959), Ichikawa depicted the abandonment and decimation of Japanese troops leading up to and following the surrender of August 1945. Given the ongoing divisiveness in Japan regarding the memorialization of the Pacific War, these are not only monumental antiwar films; they also signal the vagaries of ideological contradiction surrounding this history.

*The Burmese Harp* and *Fires on the Plain* are very different films, based on novels by different authors. Kon Ichikawa had a remarkably wide range of tones and styles that he employed throughout his career (77 films from 1945 to 2001). Particularly known for his adaptation of literary classics such as Mishima's *The Golden Pavilion* (*Enjo*, 1958) and Tanizaki's *The Key* (*Kagi*, 1959), he also proved himself to be an exemplary documentary filmmaker with *Tokyo Olympiad* (1965). Although he was not as "political" as some of the New Wave filmmakers, Ichikawa had a strong sense of irony that gives his best films a subversive edge. It is this sardonic streak that distinguishes *Fires on the Plain* as one of the most powerful treatments of war in world cinema, at once absurd and surreal, with documentary-like authenticity. *The Burmese Harp*, on the other hand, eschews irony for sentimentality.

The literary original of *The Burmese Harp* was written by Michio Takeyama in 1946, when the shock of surrender still needed to be absorbed by the Japanese public. Takeyama's novel, which was originally published in serial form, served as a kind of healing balm made up of equal parts spiritual syrup, colonial fantasy and boys-club militarism. Although Ichikawa had made 26 features since 1945, this was the first to bring the 41-year-old director national and international recognition (the two often go hand in hand in Japan) when it won the prestigious San Giorgio Prize at Venice. The film's interest today is primarily as a document of the Japanese struggle to memorialize the war dead.

The central conceit of *The Burmese Harp* is that music can bridge cultural difference and create bonds between warring groups. Mizushima (Shoji Yasui) is a soldier in a squad led by a choral master, Captain Inouye (Rentaro Mikuni), who leads his men in song and in battle. Shortly after the film opens, however, the end of the war is announced and the squad begins a retreat to the city of Mudon. Mizushima has mastered the art of the Burmese harp to accompany his harmonizing comrades, and it is he who is selected to persuade another squad, barricaded in cavernous mountains, to surrender to the Allied troops. He fails in his mission and witnesses the stubborn suicidal destruction of the embattled squadron. Separated from his own squad, Mizushima becomes a Buddhist monk, and the bulk of the film concerns his wanderings through the desolate war-torn landscape. His comrades, hospitably kept as prisoners of war (POWs) by the British, try to locate him, but Mizushima finally chooses not to make contact, nor to return to Japan, but to stay in Burma to bury the fallen Japanese soldiers.

Unfortunately, neither Ichikawa nor Takeyama made much of an effort to incorporate elements of Burmese culture. Mizushima's hand-held stringed harp, which Ichikawa admits now is little more than a prop, is incongruously synchronized with a multi-stringed orchestral instrument. Moreover, the film's

**Fig. 50** Shoji Yasui in *The Burmese Harp* (Ichikawa, 1956).

theme song, intoned repeatedly by the singing soldiers, is a Japanese version of the British/American folk song "Home! Sweet Home!" By the 1950s this had become adapted as a popular Japanese song called "Hanyo no yado." Thus, the rousing choral collaboration among Japanese, American and British troops has nothing to do with Burma and everything to do with the cultural unification of Japan with its former Allied enemies in Southeast Asia.

Ichikawa may have tried to make an "adult movie" from a children's fairy-tale novel, but the result remains a fantasy of colonial redemption. The Burmese iconography is strictly background scenery and Mizushima's conversion to monkhood is little more than a means for him to gain respect from the local peasants. He steals a cloak from a monk and, once in disguise, gradually undergoes a spiritual awakening as he discovers the bodies of abandoned Japanese soldiers strewn across the landscape. Despite the platitudes that Burma is Buddha's own land, Mizushima's conversion is a deeply nationalist one. In full Buddhist monk regalia, he salutes a burial mound of his fallen comrades; he carries a Japanese-style white box of ashes in a procession with other monks, marking his difference alongside his spiritual identity.

The black-and-white landscape cinematography is for many commentators the chief asset of *The Burmese Harp*; and yet, compared with *Fires on the Plain* and many other Japanese films of the 1950s, its compositions tend to be clichéd and derivative. Shot almost exclusively in Japan, the many long-shot tableaux of mountains, rivers and beaches are based on conventions of Western and Chinese landscape painting. In many ways, the film demonstrates Ichikawa's background in animation and his admiration of Walt Disney. What is remarkable about *The Burmese Harp* is how he has borrowed the visual and musical styles of Anglo colonialism to make "peace" with Burma.

*The Burmese Harp* is unambiguously about the repatriation of Japanese soldiers and their remorse for those left behind. The ravaged Burmese landscape, still studded with ancient temples and religious sites (Ichikawa did shoot some touristy footage with the lead actor in Burma), is effectively transformed into a memorial site, while the fate of the Burmese people and their casualties is essentially and absolutely effaced. To be sure, the depiction of the Japanese squad refusing to surrender constituted an important critical gesture in postwar Japan, and the heaps of bodies, although they are merely glimpsed, points unambiguously to the evils of war. As a variety of "humanism," however, the

**Fig. 51** *The Burmese Harp* (Ichikawa, 1956).

film's message of pacifism remains cloaked in the rhetoric of nationalism, colonialism and cultural imperialism.

The category of postwar humanism in 1950s Japan actually includes quite a number of variations. Ichikawa's return to the desperate scene of Southeast Asia in *Fires on the Plain* is so much more bleak, ironic and grotesque that it hardly seems the work of the same director. The black-and-white cinematography is equally stylized, but in this film it is far more expressionistic and dynamic. There may be no other war film that depicts the litter of human bodies quite like *Fires on the Plain*. They scatter the Philippine frontier like strange growths. Scenes of bodies falling in mud, patients crawling from a hospital under attack, bodies strewn over hillsides and craters; this is the landscape through which Tamura (Eiji Funakoshi) wanders. In the opening scene, he is ejected from his company because he has tuberculosis, and then evicted from the hospital as he is not sick enough. In fact neither faction wants to feed him; he is given a grenade and some yams and left to fend for himself.

Shohei Ooka's novel was based on his own wartime experiences as a soldier and POW, and *Fires on the Plain* comes much closer than *The Burmese Harp* to the reality of war, depicting the abandonment of Japanese troops 6 months before the August 1945 defeat. Ichikawa and his screenwriter wife, Natto Wada, eliminated the discourse of Christianity from the original, leaving a narrative with no redemption. The fires of the title refer to plumes of smoke that Tamura sees from time to time rising from distant plains. He is told they belong to farmers burning corn husks, as Japanese farmers burn rice hulls, and it is toward this image of ritual purification that Tamura staggers at the end of the film before he falls in a hail of bullets. It hardly matters if he lives or dies after what he has gone through, and the fire — glimpsed in close-up moments before he collapses — is little more than an allegory of redemption. That the image of home is also an image of conflagration is emblematic of the film's twisted ironies.

Tamura scares himself by shooting a Filipina in an abandoned village, and afterwards he throws his rifle in the river in a gesture of renunciation, but he is still in a war zone. At the dark heart of the film, Tamura encounters Nagamatsu (Micky Curtis) and his commanding officer Yasuda (Osamu Takizawa) who trade tobacco and "monkey meat" with the stream of men stumbling along an impassable road. Monkey meat is inevitably revealed to be a euphemism for cannibalism, to which Tamura almost succumbs, except that his teeth fall out from scurvy. He seems to be beyond remorse, as his struggle for survival has taken him to the limits of his humanity. In this film, the only reference to Buddhist transcendence is articulated by a crazed soldier perched under a tree, eating dirt.

*Fires on the Plain* succeeds primarily due to Funakoshi's clown-like performance. Funakoshi was a Daiei studio regular who, Ichikawa says, starved himself to play the role of Tamura — to the point where he collapsed from malnutrition and halted the production for 2 months. Funakoshi's bow-legged unsoldierly walk is a Chaplin conceit, and his deadpan stare could be likewise borrowed from Buster Keaton. This is the crux of Ichikawa's humanism in this film. Tamura is at the bottom, the last survivor, the man who survives only by recognizing his station on the lowest rung. Thus the infamous scene in which a successive series of men upgrade their boots in a muddy rainstorm, leaving Tamura to finally pick up a pair without soles, is at once ridiculous, but fitting. He looks through the bottom of the shoe with a wide-eyed look of resignation, and then happily squishes his toes in the mud, proceeding barefoot but more content than those who went before.

**Fig. 52** Eiji Funakoshi in *Fires on the Plain* (Ichikawa, 1959).

As Chuck Stephens notes in his essay in the Criterion package, *Fires on the Plain*, despite its agonizing depiction of war, still manages to evade the larger picture of the Japanese campaign in the Philippines. By 1959 it was no secret that cannibalism and many other atrocities had been committed in New Guinea and the Philippines. Top Japanese officers had been executed for war crimes, and yet this national humiliation had more or less remained invisible in popular culture. Ichikawa cannily keeps his protagonist from indulging in cannibalism himself, but Tamura's violent encounter with a romantic young couple, ending with the Filipina's death, registers a kind of brutality that suggests on an individual level what might have taken place more generally. The film may shy away from full disclosure, but it certainly enters more deeply into this grotesque history than any mainstream Japanese film has before or since.

A well-known fact of Ichikawa's biography, recapitulated in his interview in the *Fires on the Plain* disk, is that his family survived the bombing of Hiroshima. In many ways, the ravaged landscapes of *The Burmese Harp* and *Fires on the Plain*, with their heaps of stinking corpses, are more evocative of the devastation that took place on Japanese soil than anything else. In fact, both films were largely shot in Izu and Hakone, popular resort regions of Japan. If the Japanese landscape is made to stand in for Southeast Asia, the casualties overseas in both films are those of Japanese troops. Each film in its own way confronts the dark side of the Pacific War without acknowledging the real damage that was done to occupied lands and peoples. Japanese politicians today remain unable to fully confront the historical record, and it is especially in this context that the horrific achievement of *Fires on the Plain* should be recognized as an existential treatise rather than a historical document.

Eastwood's return to this difficult history 50 years later predictably supplies a reluctant hero in the person of General Kuribayashi (Ken Watanabe).

**Fig. 53** Eiji Funakoshi in *Fires on the Plain* (Ichikawa, 1959).

Ichikawa's films are based mainly on the figure in the landscape, rather than psychological portraits (in fact, another element removed from Ooka's novel is the perspective from the mental hospital where the author locates himself after the war). The character of Saito in *Letters from Iwo Jima* might be taken as a kind of recapitulation of Ichikawa's protagonists Mizushima and Tamura, enlisted men who are witnesses to an unspeakable national casualty. Ichikawa's two films are linked by their deployment of the "common man" protagonist — an archetype of Hollywood cinema. *Letters* was very popular in Japan in turn because it provided an intimate perspective to which a new generation of viewers could relate.

One of the recurring events in these three films is the attempts of individual soldiers to surrender to Allied troops, and the motif is emblematic of the confusion facing men on the front lines when the war turned against the Japanese. The scenario of surrender in all three films ends badly. In *Fires on the Plain* a soldier attempts to surrender to the Americans, only to be shot by a Filipina soldier in a hysterical burst of vengeful gunfire. A similar plight befalls one of Saito's colleagues in *Letters*. In *The Burmese Harp*, Mizushima's surrender (he waves the white flag, although none of the men appear to follow him) leads ultimately to the complete surrender of his national identity. His refusal of repatriation becomes his badge of honor, but by becoming a monk he idealistically transcends the divisions between nations and cultures. We could say much the same of Eastwood's attempt to understand and represent a former enemy of the United States in *Letters*, in which Kuribayashi is himself an idealized figure — a Japanese general sympathetic to Americans. *Fires on the Plain*, on the other hand, depicts war as an existential horror for which no amount of ideological whitewashing can provide explanation or solace.

## *THE HUMAN CONDITION*: THE ENDLESS POSTWAR

Weighing in at 9.5 hours, *The Human Condition* ranks among the longest and most ambitious epics of world cinema. Respecting the detail of the six-volume novel by Junpei Gomikawa, director Masaki Kobayashi and his co-screenwriter Zenzo Matsuyama even shot several scenes that didn't make the final cut. Gumikawa's epic was broadcast as a radio drama before being filmed and, by 1959, 2.5 million copies of the book had been sold in Japan.[4] The powerful war story constitutes one of the most searing criticisms of the Japanese role in the Pacific War, and while its sheer weight may help to amplify and deepen its critique, the poetry is spread just a little thin in Kobayashi's long-winded adaptation.

Originally released as three separate films, each with two parts, the full-length version is and was often shown in one continuous six-part screening. The protagonist Kaji, played by Tatsuya Nakadai, anchors the whole film, filtering the ideological and physical struggle of the war through a psychological portrayal of liberal humanism. The film inevitably supports the postwar discourse of individualism, and yet as the character undergoes significant changes due to the shifting circumstances of the war so too does the cinematography and film style. The three separate films follow upon one another chronologically and yet, aesthetically, they are also three distinct films.

**Fig. 54** Tatsuya Nakadai in *The Human Condition* (Kobayashi, 1959–61).

The setting is not the Pacific at all, but Manchuria and its border with the USSR. Shot entirely in Hokkaido, the huge northern island of the Japanese archipelago, the landscapes throughout the film are dramatic, ranging from dense jungle to snowy fields, but are most often desolate and barren. The film's widescreen black-and-white compositions emphasize an endless deserted horizon, over which lies the future, the past and the unknown. The last two parts of the film, bracketed together as "A Soldier's Prayer" in which Kaji is abandoned by a defeated army, are by far the strongest cinematically. Kaji is constantly moving, picking up an assortment of companions along the way, both soldiers and Japanese civilians who are likewise stranded and hunted by both the revengeful Chinese peasants and the Soviet army. In fact, the Soviets did not attack the Japanese until after the bombing of Hiroshima and Nagasaki, so the combat scenes in the film — of which there are only about 20 minutes, in part four — take place after the official surrender, which no one in the field seems to know about. The Japanese officers fight suicidally to the death, while Kaji struggles on with a relentless will for survival.

Kobayashi himself was drafted into the army and, despite his university education, refused to be promoted to officer status as a form of resistance to the military machine. Both he and author Gumikawa spent time in POW camps, and Kaji's character is developed out of their experiences as unwilling participants in a brutal and sadistic military environment. Kaji starts off as a leftist intellectual who accepts a posting in Manchuria as a labor supervisor in exchange for an exemption from military service. He fruitlessly, yet relentlessly, attempts to introduce humane methods to the supervision of the Chinese conscripted labor force mining coal in the open-pit wastelands of the Japanese colony. His attempts at reform are repeatedly foiled by a fascist administration that is not only brutal but also conniving and duplicitous. He is finally framed for allowing conscripts to escape and he is subsequently forced into military service.

This first film, entitled "No Greater Love," is strangely static, with long scenes played out with little movement. The Chinese extras are filmed in lines, blocks and groups that in long shot form stylized patterns of figures against the barren landscape. Their movements are frequently synchronized, so that the film style ironically aligns itself with what Sontag famously described as a fascist aesthetic. In conjunction with the didacticism of Kaji's humanist insistence on nonviolent methods, this first portion of the epic painfully dramatizes the impotence of the protagonist's liberal views.

To make matters worse, Kaji's wife, Michiko (Michiyo Aratama), who has accompanied him to Manchuria, is a simpering and frankly unsympathetic character. While he struggles against the fascist machine, she begs and whines for him to stay home and not get involved. She becomes symbolic in the film of an idealized notion of "Japan before the war" that Kaji longs to return to. After he is drafted, she appears frequently in flashback, and she is inexplicably allowed to see him at his training camp for a conjugal visit — after which he is savagely beaten by the very men who authorized the visit.

*The Human Condition* is in fact somewhat preoccupied with sexuality, suggesting a deep link between violence and sexual repression. The Japanese officials at the labor camp have Kaji bring in Chinese comfort women to keep the POWs in line, and one of them, played by Chikage Awashima, spies for the Kempeitai — the Japanese military police. In his subsequent wanderings across Manchuria, Kaji seems to constantly attract women, including a nurse and a series of women in desperate situations (Kyoko Kishida, Hideko Takamine), although he remains faithful to his memory of Michiko. His compatriots are not always so friendly though, and both the Japanese and the Soviets take advantage of Japanese women in the lawless world of the abandoned front. While rape is the prevalent and permanent danger, some women also use sex strategically for survival. At one point, Kaji's beleaguered band of soldiers are taken in by a barn full of women who "comfort" them in an orgy of squirming bodies. Despite its humanism, the film ultimately makes no apologies for the role of comfort women, but deftly incorporates them into its liberal-humanist agenda.

The repression of homosociality, meanwhile, is rampant in the military rituals of humiliation, in which conscripts are forced into the roles of prostitutes, and in drinking games in which men take the roles of singing-and-dancing geisha. In fact the film is extraordinarily detailed in its portrayal of military rituals, hierarchies, double standards and Kafkaesque plots. The second film of the trilogy, "The Road to Eternity," is devoted mainly to Kaji's military training, for which the actors themselves received rigorous training for an accurate portrayal of military regimen. As a portrait of fascist protocol, the film is painfully realistic, covering a whole series of institutions, including a military hospital, the colonial mining operation, the POW camps and their railway-building operations, ad hoc field camps run by rogue officers, along with the rigorous routines of basic training. Kaji continues to chafe against these institutional structures, even while he is gradually indoctrinated into the machine as he proves himself to be a skilled marksman and a natural leader, adapting against his will to a culture of violence.

*The Human Condition* details the lesser-known context of the last humiliation of the Japanese army. By 1945, Manchuria was a backwater in the larger contest, and was staffed mainly by the last wave of recruits, many of them older men and upstart rich kids whose exemptions had run out. Purged of officers and armaments that had been redirected to the main theater of war, it was a lean and badly equipped force that was finally trampled by the Soviet tanks. Within this vacuum of leadership, Kaji's moral integrity is further challenged as he fights for survival. The big battle scene, in which the military hierarchy dissolves, leaving the survivors in disarray, picks up the pace of the film and initiates Kaji's desperate wanderings that comprise the last two parts of the film.

As early as part two, Kaji is bitterly disillusioned with his own nation, stating bluntly, "It's not my fault that I'm Japanese, yet it's my worst crime that I am." However, the greater disillusionment of *The Human Condition* is with Stalinism. Repeatedly accused of being a "Red" by the Kempeitai, Kaji believes that the Soviets will be his salvation, and that some kind of great paradise lies over the next range of mountains. The enemy does not appear in person until part six. Huge Soviet soldiers accompanied by Chinese peasant allies are rounding up POWs and Kaji himself is finally forced to surrender in order to save the aforementioned barn-full of Japanese women from being killed. In the Soviet POW camp, the Japanese are inevitably treated like animals: starved, overworked and humiliated. They are reduced to scavenging for table scraps from the camp's garbage heaps, and Kaji's hopes for humane treatment from his idols are crudely ruined.

**Fig. 55** Ronald Self, Ed Keene and Tatsuya Nakadai in *The Human Condition* (Kobayashi, 1959–61).

Kaji attempts to plead his case with the authorities, who dismiss him as a "fascist samurai." His Kempeitai interpreter fails to communicate his ideological sympathies with the Soviet officers in one of the film's most moving scenes. The linguistic morass, complicated by the Kempeitai's unreliability, currying favor with the Soviets, pits ideology against survival. However, somehow in the exchange with a secondary benevolent comrade standing under a huge portrait of Stalin, the resulting punishment is not Siberia, but a mere week of hard labor.

It is not clear whether Kaji's pronouncement that "the fact that socialism is better than fascism is not enough to keep us alive," has been fully understood by the Soviets or not. The melodrama of misunderstanding finally redeems the more predictable melodrama of the suffering war victim.

*The Human Condition* is punctuated by epigrammatic lines of dialogue as Kaji negotiates the shifting tides of postwar ideologies. One of the more striking such aphorisms comes after Kaji is driven to the cold-blooded murder of a Soviet sentry: "What we need is a defeated man's code, not a soldier's code." Kaji's idealistic motivation for continued survival is to return "to our former lives," and yet the film is equally explicit about the impossibility of such a return. It is distinct among postwar Japanese films about the war in that Kaji rejects the identity of a victim, to become a tragic hero. He exemplifies the suffering and privations of the war experience, but also transcends them through his endurance and willingness to stand up to a long series of aggressive military personnel. Absorbing the brutality of the imperialist war machine for the sake of survival, our protagonist is faced also with the loss of his socialist ideals. The film thus falls in line with the Cold War policies introduced to Japan in the American Occupation, even though the role of the United States is entirely absent from the film.

The critique of socialism is in the end far less harsh than the critique of Japanese imperialism. There may have been no Americans in the film and yet it was one of the few postwar films to include the world outside Japan, and to include Chinese and Soviet characters, even if they are played mainly by Japanese and Americans respectively. It is both surprising and rewarding to hear Nakadai and many of the other Japanese actors speaking fairly good Mandarin Chinese in their roles as labor overseers in the first third of the film.

The Criterion package includes several excellent interviews. Director Mitsuhiro Shinoda interviews Kobayashi and also offers his own insightful analysis of the film in a separate interview. A very elegant-looking Tatsuya Nakadai is also interviewed. He explains that this was his first leading role, in a film that was shot chronologically over a 4-year period. Working with many of the leading stars of the period, including So Yamamura, Chikage Awashima, Keiji Sada and Hideko Takamine, Nakadai learned a great deal about acting over the course of the production, and it shows. At the outset, his psychological dilemmas are portrayed simply by an unblinking stare; by the last installment, his voice has dropped an octave and he moves with more grace and fluidity. He looks stronger and more confident once he grows a beard, and his maturity extends to his body language. In the midst of the chaos and desperation of the abandoned military front, Kaji eschews a mystical authority that gains him instant respect from his compatriots despite his lack of rank, as if by sheer force of personality.

Both Kobayashi and Shinoda are eloquent about the contributions of cinematographer Yoshio Miyajima, who was apparently a "hard-core communist." Kobayashi was concerned about offending him with the film's critique of the Soviet handling of POWs, but he evidently swallowed his pride. The remarkable stylistic shifts, from the highly stylized aesthetics of the first film to the military war maneuvers of the second to the relentless walking of the third film, gives the epic a varied visual vocabulary that matches Kaji's evolution as a character. The early scenes are much more brightly lit, set in the wide open space of the desolate mine, while the very last scenes in the Soviet camp are set mainly at night or in windowless barracks.

Kaji's final desperate escape includes a sequence in which he takes on a Christlike aura, dressed in torn burlap over his wrecked uniform. Burdened with a sack of sand on his shoulder, he joins up with a work force but collapses under its weight as if it were a cross, as if he were carrying the sins of his nation. At this point he has become delusional, hallucinating images of food as he crosses one empty landscape after another, until he finally collapses in the snow; it is as if the film itself finally relinquishes its realist agenda for the sake of a martyr's death. Nakadai struggles on with his trademark blank stare, conversing hysterically with his faraway wife Michiko. Meanwhile, Miyajima's magnificent landscape shots, in which Kaji's small figure is alone in a series of shifting horizons, gives the ending its emotional weight.

The opening and closing credits of each of the three parts of *The Human Condition* feature a curious relief frieze of "primitive" figures of men and women. The film may aspire to reveal the basic conditions of what it is to be human, and yet its interest and significance lies more specifically in its treatment of the Japanese wartime experience. Like most professed antiwar films, its critique is inevitably compromised by its depiction of war itself — in this case, the portrait of heroism and military survival. Kaji may not be a willing participant in the war but, once in its grasp, he excels as a sharpshooter and humane authority

figure. In this sense, the film is able to provide a portrait of the Japanese soldier that meets the criteria of postwar humanism, while memorializing and
commemorating the war dead. The huge popularity of the source novel and
the film itself in Japan points to its role in Japan's difficult postwar acceptance
of defeat.

The ideological project of *The Human Condition* is ostensibly a negotiation
of fascism and communism, conveniently replacing the "democratic" Cold War
agenda of the Occupation with a more vague notion of liberal humanism. But
Kaji ends up falling alone with his loss of country, without the defeated man's
code he vainly seeks. The film's critique of fascism and denunciation of the cruel
treatment of the Chinese during the long occupation of Manchuria nevertheless
remains unmatched in Japanese film history.

The last 10 years has seen a revival of neo-nationalism in Japan, exemplified
by the graphic novels of another Kobayashi (Yoshinori) whose best-selling "war
debate" (a.k.a. *Neo Gomanism Manifesto*) revives the anti-Western agenda of
the imperialist mandate. Given the serious lack of comprehensive historical
educational materials in Japan, the *manga*, like this epic film of the early 1960s,
is hugely influential on how the wartime past is framed for young audiences.
In this light, despite its didacticism and individualism, its romanticization of
feminine domesticity and its pretentious length, *The Human Condition* marks
a high point in the Japanese cultural memory of the 1937–45 war. Its effec-
tive ideological postwar project is to blur the distinction between those who
opposed the war and those who fought valiantly and unsuccessfully under the
imperial banner. In fact there is no postwar in *The Human Condition*, which
tells the story of a war that has no end,[5] and, indeed, as long as its significance
is still under debate, the postwar may not have ended yet.

# Conclusion

The "big four" Japanese directors featured in this book — Ozu, Mizoguchi, Kurosawa and Naruse — are not necessarily representative of the entire spectrum of styles and genres comprised by the classical Japanese cinema. Dozens of other directors played crucial roles in developing the recognizable idiom of this 30-year period. These four directors, however, were recognized by their peers, by the industry, by critics and by Japanese audiences as being on the top rung of a fairly hierarchical system of production. This is further evident from their repeated rankings in *Kinema Junpo* top-ten lists, and by the testimonies of actors and crew who held them in great regard. In the cases of Kurosawa and Mizoguchi, their status was further solidified by their international recognition. The fact that the films of these four directors have been made available to English-speaking audiences before those of their contemporaries (albeit in a limited way, especially in the case of Naruse) is in keeping with their prestige in Japan.

Ichikawa and Kobayashi emerged in the 1950s as members of a new generation of directors roughly contemporary with Kurosawa. They worked in a variety of genres and were not as strongly tied to an authorial style as the "big four"; in this sense they are more typical of the dozens of other directors who worked during this period. Criterion and other companies have released a handful of titles from the classical period in addition to those covered here, including *Crazed Fruit* (Ko Nakahira, 1956) and a package of five Nikkatsu Noir titles from the late 1950s and early 1960s. These films are important precursors to the New Wave cinema that eclipsed the classical era in the 1960s. By the end of the 1950s, Japanese cinema was already deeply affected by the dynamic energy of the new counterculture that refused to buy into what was perceived as a staid classicism.

As for the early part of the classical period, at the time of writing Criterion has released two additional Ozu titles and three of Naruse's silent films. There is also a box set of films by Hiroshi Shimizu made between 1933 and 1941, including one silent film, *Japanese Girls at the Harbor* (1933). Shimizu's style combines the long-take deep-focus tendencies of Mizoguchi's filmmaking with the *shoshimin-eiga* feeling of Ozu and Naruse. His cinema is notable for its "wandering" homelessness and his interest in people in transit, outside the family system that anchors so much of the *gendai-geki* cinema of the classical era. Shimizu's narrative style is likewise episodic and elliptical, set in rural locations in which landscape is featured prominently. He shares with his colleagues a realist aesthetic that extends to a form of narrative that is consistently open at the end, inviting the spectator to speculate about what might happen next.

The open-endedness of classical Japanese cinema is what most consistently distinguishes it from classical Hollywood cinema. The closure of American cinema is one of the recurring features that has made it an object of such disdain. Due to the routine endings, often enforced by censorship, in which the guilty are punished and/or the lovers unite, American cinema of the studio era has tended to be interpreted as a closed system. Its codes of narrative realism are said to be governed by hard and fast rules of continuity editing, and its moral authority tends to uphold the status quo.[1] In fact, the homogeneity of classical Hollywood cinema and the tightness of its codes of representation can and have been questioned by film scholars and challenged by filmmakers.[2] In my view, classical Hollywood is a rich and dynamic cinema with great variety, and the films remain open to multiple readings, but this may not be the place to develop that argument.

Classical Japanese cinema is often considered to be aesthetically "different" because of its openness, although we should also note that American censors during the Occupation ensured that Japanese cinema likewise ended on upbeat happy endings and that due punishment was meted out to gangsters and villains. Wartime censorship was equally heavy-handed on issues of morality; and even after the Occupation, producers and censors had tremendous say over representations of sexuality and gender roles. However, the vast majority of films produced during the studio era of Japanese cinema, and most of those discussed in this book, end on notes of ambivalence and ambiguity. The Zen aesthetic of *mono no aware* persists in this cinema in its consistent tone of resignation and perpetual sense of loss. The typically ambivalent ending is only one of many formal features that distinguish classical Japanese cinema from classical Hollywood cinema, although none of them can be found systematically across the board. These include violations of continuity editing, narrative ellipses and stylized visual compositions.

For all the "Japaneseness" of classical Japanese cinema, there is an equal amount of film style borrowed from the Hollywood model, including not only continuity editing but also the use of comedy, dramatic pacing, naturalistic performance styles, lighting and soundtrack. These constitute the basic vocabulary of narrative cinema. In the Japanese case, we may note a high degree of aesthetic realism that tends to support the more stylistic flourishes that directors such as Kurosawa and Ozu refined. Japanese directors were particularly skilled at creating expressive atmospheres for their stories, using weather, architecture, lighting and music for full expressive effect. This sensual, emotional use of cinematic materials, combined with an impressive roster of dynamic and expressive actors, give the films an intensity that has rendered them "classics." The use of Japanese literature as the basis of so many films further accounts for the way that entertainment and art were so closely aligned.

For all its classicism, though, classical Japanese cinema also helped to define the terms of the modern nation in terms of gender and the experience of everyday life. The pivot point of 1945, and the ideological reversals that the nation experienced through the 15 years of war and 7 years of Occupation were negotiated on numerous levels, but the cinema is arguably one of the most prominent, given its national scope and international reach. The "meaning" of modernity underwent constant change from 1930 to 1960, but, beyond intellectual circles, cinematic narrative enabled Japanese cultural producers and audiences to explore the dynamics of family, desire, subjectivity and nationhood. The aesthetic vocabulary of narrative cinema, combined with the genres of storytelling that evolved within the popular culture of the twentieth century, enabled classical Japanese cinema to engage with modernity on multiple levels. At the same time, it provided an important vehicle for Japanese culture on the international stage. In the global marketplace of the phantasmagoria — cinephiliac film culture — classical Japanese cinema continues to play a fundamental role.

# Notes

*Chapter One: The Classical, the Modern and Japanese Cinema in the Global System*

1  The key influential text in this regard is Noël Burch, *To the Distant Observer: Form and Meaning in the Japanese Cinema*. Critiques of this work have been multiple, but perhaps the most sustained and updated can be found in Mitsuhiro Yoshimoto, *Kurosawa: Film Studies and Japanese Cinema*.
2  Joseph L. Anderson and Donald Richie, *The Japanese Film: Art and Industry*, 456.
3  See, for example, Ben Singer, *Melodrama and Modernity*; and Linda Williams, "Discipline and Fun," 351–70.
4  Miriam Hansen, "The Mass Production of the Senses: Classical Cinema as Vernacular Modernism," 332–50.
5  Christine Gledhill, "Rethinking Genre," 221–43; Linda Williams, *Playing the Race Card: Melodramas of Black and White from Uncle Tom to O. J. Simpson*.
6  Eric Cazdyn, *The Flash of Capital: Film and Geopolitics in Japan*, 55.
7  Ibid., 87.
8  Naoki Sakai, "'You Asians': On the Historical Role of the West and Asia Binary," 175.
9  Ibid., 175.
10  Hansen, "Mass Production of the Senses," 335.
11  Ibid., 333.
12  Ibid., 333.
13  See Aaron Gerow, "The Word Before the Image: Criticism, the Screenplay and the Regulation of Meaning in Prewar Japanese Film Culture," 3–35.

14 Aaron Gerow, *Visions of Japanese Modernity: Articulations of Cinema, Nation, and Spectatorship, 1895–1925,* 223.

15 Ibid., 226.

16 Darell William Davis, *Picturing Japaneseness: Monumental Style, National Identity, Japanese Film.*

17 Sharon H. Hayashi, "Traveling Film History: Language and Landscape in the Japanese Cinema, 1931–45," 11.

18 Ibid., 32.

19 Ibid., 11.

20 Ibid., 192.

21 Hansen, "Mass Production of the Senses," 339.

22 Cazdyn, *The Flash of Capital,* 73.

23 For a good discussion of the vicissitudes of classical cinema arguments, see Robert B. Ray, "The Bordwell Regime and the Stakes of Knowledge," 29–63.

24 David Bordwell, Janet Staiger and Kristin Thompson, *The Classical Hollywood Cinema: Film Style and Mode of Production to 1960,* 4.

25 André Bazin, *What Is Cinema?,* 29.

26 Harry Harootunian, "'Detour to the East': Noël Burch and the Task of Japanese Film," 7–8.

27 Anderson and Richie, *Japanese Film,* 393.

28 Miriam Hansen, "Fallen Women, Rising Stars, New Horizons: Shanghai Silent Film as Vernacular Modernism," 10–22, 19.

29 *I Lived, But . . .* by Kazuo Inoue, 1983, distributed by Criterion Collection with *Tokyo Story* DVD; and *Kenji Mizoguchi: The Life of a Film Director,* directed by Kaneto Shindo, 1975, distributed by Criterion Collection with *Ugetsu* DVD; Teruyo Nogami, *Waiting on the Weather: Making Movies with Akira Kurosawa.*

30 Williams, *Playing the Race Card,* 22.

31 Gledhill, "Rethinking Genre," 221–43.

32 Williams, *Playing the Race Card,* 23.

33 The term "moral legibility" is taken from Peter Brooks's influential theory of melodrama, *The Melodramatic Imagination: Balzac, Henry James, Melodrama, and the Mode of Excess.* In her discussion of melodrama as the dominant mode of American cinema in *Playing the Race Card,* Linda Williams uses this term extensively. She argues that it is more appropriate than Brooks's more commonly cited term "moral occult" to use in "the face of an increasingly secular, atomized and commodified culture," 25, 315.

34 Peter Brooks, 49.

35 Mitsuhiro Yoshimoto, "Logic of Sentiment: The Postwar Japanese Cinema and Questions of Modernity," 30.

36  Ibid., 30.
37  Gledhill, "Rethinking Genre," 227.
38  Ibid., 235.
39  M. Madhava Prasad, *Ideology of the Hindi Film: A Historical Construction*, 62.
40  Ibid., 78.
41  Gledhill, "Rethinking Genre," 229.
42  Kinnia Yau Shuk-ting, "Interactions between Japanese and Hong Kong Action Cinemas," 36.
43  Ibid., 43.
44  Rob Wilson, "Spectral Critiques: Tracking 'Uncanny' Filmic Paths Towards a Bio-Poetics of Trans-Pacific Globalization," 268.
45  David Bordwell, *Planet Hong Kong: Popular Cinema and the Art of Entertainment*, 82. Quoted by Wilson, 264.
46  Hye Seung Chung, "Toward a Strategic Korean Cinephilia: A Transnational Détournement of Hollywood Melodrama," 120.
47  Ibid., 140.
48  Wimal Dissanayake, ed., *Melodrama and Asian Cinema*.
49  Mitsuhiro Yoshimoto, "Melodrama, Postmodernism and Japanese Cinema," 121.
50  Chung, "Toward a Strategic Korean Cinephilia," 120–1.


*Chapter Two: Yasujiro Ozu*

1  David Bordwell, *Ozu and the Poetics of Cinema*; Donald Richie, *Ozu*. For a very different approach, see Kiju Yoshida, *Ozu's Anti-Cinema*.
2  Bordwell, *Ozu and the Poetics of Cinema*.
3  Mitsuyo Wada-Marciano, *Nippon Modern: Japanese Cinema of the 1920s and 1930s*, 5.
4  Donald Richie, Audio Commentary on *Story of Floating Weeds* Criterion DVD.
5  Marilyn Ivy, *Discourses of the Vanishing: Modernity, Phantasm, Japan*, 192–240.
6  Bordwell, *Ozu and the Poetics of Cinema*, 256–9.


*Chapter Three: Kenji Mizoguchi and his Women*

1  Carole Cavanaugh, "'Sanchô Dayû' and the Overthrow of History," 19.

*Chapter Four: Men with Swords and Men with Suits*

1   Donald Richie, foreword in Teruyo Nogami, *Waiting on the Weather: Making Movies with Akira Kurosawa*, 8.
2   Stuart Galbraith IV, *The Emperor and the Wolf*, 57–63.
3   Ibid., 57.
4   Mitsuhiro Yoshimoto, *Kurosawa: Film Studies and Japanese Cinema*, 2.
5   Galbraith, *The Emperor and the Wolf*, 220.
6   Ibid., 121.
7   Ibid., 389.
8   Gilles Deleuze, *Cinema One: The Movement Image*, 188.
9   Galbraith, *The Emperor and the Wolf*, 354.
10   Deleuze, 189.
11   Gilles Deleuze, *Cinema One: The Movement Image*, 188.
12   Stephen Prince, 174.
13   Galbraith, *The Emperor and the Wolf*, 194.
14   Ibid., 388.
15   Yoshimoto, *Kurosawa*, 338.


*Chapter Five: Mikio Naruse*

1   Joan Ericson, *Be a Woman: Hayashi Fumiko and Modern Japanese Women's Literature*, 85.
2   Laura Mulvey, "Notes on Sirk and Melodrama," 75–9.
3   Interview with Toshiro Ide, Hide Murakawa, *Naruse Mikio Enshutsujutsu: Yakusha ga kataru engi no genba*, 164.
4   Takao Toda, review of *Meshi* (*A Married Life*, a.k.a. *Repast*) *Eiga Hyoron* (January 1952): 85–6, trans. Guy Yasko.
5   Mulvey, "Notes," 79.
6   Juzaburo Futaba, "Review of *Meshi*," *Kinema Junpo*, 116.
7   Chiyota Shimizu, "Review of *Meshi* (*Repast*)," 43.
8   Toda Takao, *Meshi* (*Repast*), *Eiga Hyōron*, January 1952, pp. 8–6.
9   Ericson, *Be a Woman*, 103–6.
10   Interview with Toshiro Ide, Murakawa, *Naruse Mikio Enshutsujutsu*, 164.
11   Yasunari Kawabata, *The Sound of the Mountain*, 234.
12   Kiyo Mikawa, "*Yama no oto*: kyokan sasou yome no tachiba (*Sound of the Mountain*: Sympathy for The Status of a Daughter-in-Law)," 5.
13   Jun Takami, "Kanso [Impressions]," *Fujin Koron* (March 1954): 222, trans. Chika Kinoshita.

14  Shigehiko Hasumi, "Mikio Naruse or Double Signature," in *Mikio Naruse*, 84.

15  Freda Freiberg, interview on *Floating Clouds*, BFI DVD release.

16  Ericson, *Be a Woman*, 78.

17  Hasumi, "Mikio Naruse or Double Signature," 70.

18  Fumiko Hayashi, *Floating Clouds*.

19  Jean Douchet, "About Naruse," *Mikio Naruse*, 98.

20  In Noriko Mizuta's discussion of the novel, she says that Tomioka encounters a local woman when he climbs the mountain, leaving Yukiko sick in bed. After she dies, he goes to Kagoshima, "gets drunk, buys a prostitute and abandons himself to his feelings of loneliness." Noriko Mizuta, "In Search of a Lost Paradise: The Wandering Woman in Hayashi Fumiko's *Drifting Clouds*," 343–4.

21  Mitsuhiro Yoshimoto, "Logic of Sentiment," 47.

22  Yoshimoto, "Logic of Sentiment: The Postwar Japanese Cinema and Questions of Modernity," 48.

23  Susanna Fessler, *Wandering Heart: The Work and Method of Hayashi Fumiko*, 95.

24  Ericson, *Be a Woman*, 82.

25  Douchet, "About Naruse," 97.

26  Sanezumi Fujimoto, "Producer Sanezumi Fujimoto," in Hasumi and Yamane eds., *Mikio Naruse*, 183.

27  Hasumi, "Double Signature," 64.

28  Douchet, "About Naruse," 99.

29  Mizuta, "In Search of a Lost Paradise," 335.

30  Nicholas Bornoff, *Pink Samurai: Love, Marriage and Sex in Contemporary Japan*, 254.

31  Tadashi Iijima, "Naruse Mikio to *Onna ga kaidan o agaru toki* (Naruse Mikio and *When a Woman Ascends the Stairs*)" *Eiga Hyoron*, 39.

*Chapter Six: Remembering the War*

1  Nagisa Oshima, "The Defeated Have No Images: Had Television Existed at the End of the War," 10.

2  Mark Sandler, *The Confusion Era: Art and Culture of Japan during the Allied Occupation, 1945–52*.

3  Mitsuhiro Yoshimoto, "Logic of Sentiment: The Postwar Japanese Cinema and Questions of Modernity," 42.

4  For two excellent discussions of the place of the film and novel in Japanese

culture of the 1950s, see Naoko Shimazu, "Popular Representations of the Past: The Case of Postwar Japan," 101–16; and Sandra Wilson, "War, Soldier and Nation in 1950s Japan," 187–218.

5   The notion of the endless postwar is developed by Mitsuyo Wada-Marciano in the introduction to *Unfinished Business: The Endless Postwar in Japanese Cinema and Visual Culture*, 1–6.


## Conclusion

1   The most rigorous account of the institutional form of classic Hollywood cinema is David Bordwell, Janet Staiger, and Kristin Thompson, *The Classical Hollywood Cinema: Film Style and Mode of Production to 1960*. Noël Burch argues for the "institutional" closure of the Hollywood system in his seminal contribution to Japanese film studies, *To the Distant Observer: Form and Meaning in the Japanese Cinema*, in contrast to the openness of the Japanese system. Many critics, including Donald Richie (in *A Hundred Years of Japanese Cinema*, 11–12), have subsequently reiterated Burch's oppositional theory of the "representational" style of Hollywood, against the "presentational" style of Japanese cinema, an argument that holds only for a portion of the films produced in the 1920s and 1930s.

2   For a full discussion of theories of classical realism, see Christopher Williams, "After the Classic, the Classical and Ideology: The Differences of Realism," 206–20.

# Filmography

The following titles are all available in various formats and regions, but I have listed those that are discussed in each chapter, with the details of the DVD releases that were used for this book.

*Chapter Two: Yasujiro Ozu*

*An Autumn Afternoon* [*Sanma no aji*]. Directed by Yasujiro Ozu (color, 1962, 113 minutes). Criterion Collection.

*Floating Weeds* [*Ukigusa*]. Directed by Yasujiro Ozu (color, 1959, 119 minutes). Criterion Collection.

*I Lived, But . . .* [*Ikite wa mita keredo — Ozu Yasujiro den*]. Directed by Kazuo Inoue (color, black and white, 1983, 123 minutes). Included in *Tokyo Story*, Criterion Collection.

*I Was Born, But . . .* [*Otona no miru ehon — Umarete wa mita keredo*]. Directed by Yasujiro Ozu (black and white, silent, 1932, 90 minutes). Included in *Three Family Comedies*, Criterion Eclipse Series.

*Late Spring* [*Banshun*]. Directed by Yasujiro Ozu (black and white, 1949, 108 minutes). Criterion Collection.

*Passing Fancy* [*Dekigokoro*]. Directed by Yasujiro Ozu (black and white, silent, 1933, 100 minutes). Included in *Three Family Comedies*, Criterion Eclipse Series.

*A Story of Floating Weeds* [*Ukigusa monogatari*]. Directed by Yasujiro Ozu (black and white, 1935, 86 minutes). Criterion Collection.

*Tokyo Chorus* [*Tokyo no korasu*]. Directed by Yasujiro Ozu (black and white, silent, 1931, 90 minutes). Included in *Three Family Comedies*, Criterion Eclipse Series.

*Tokyo-Ga*. Directed by Wim Wenders (color, black and white, 1985, 92 minutes). Included in *Late Spring*, disk released by Criterion.

*Tokyo Story* [*Tokyo monogatari*]. Directed by Yasujiro Ozu (black and white, 1953, 136 minutes). Criterion Collection.


### Chapter Three:  *Kenji Mizoguchi and his Women*

*Kenji Mizoguchi: The Life of a Film Director* [*Kenji Mizoguchi: Aru eiga-kantoku no shogai*]. Directed by Kaneto Shindo (color, 1975, 150 minutes). Included in *Ugetsu* disk released by Criterion.

*Sansho the Bailiff* [*Sansho dayu*]. Directed by Kenji Mizoguchi (black and white, 1954, 124 minutes). Criterion Collection.

*Ugetsu monogatari*. Directed by Kenji Mizoguchi (black and white, 1953, 97 minutes). Criterion Collection.


### Chapter Four:  *Men with Swords and Men with Suits*

*The Bad Sleep Well* [*Warui yatsu hodo yoku nemuru*]. Directed by Akira Kurosawa (black and white, 1960, 135 minutes). Criterion Collection.

*Dersu Uzala* [*Derusu Uzara*]. Directed by Akira Kurosawa (color, 1975, 110 minutes). Kino Video.

*Dodes'kaden* [*Dodesukaden*]. Directed by Akira Kurosawa (color, 1970, 144 minutes). Criterion Collection.

*Dreams* [*Yume*]. Directed by Akira Kurosawa (color, 1990, 119 minutes). Warner Home Video.

*Drunken Angel* [*Yoidore tenshi*]. Directed by Akira Kurosawa (black and white, 1948, 98 minutes). Criterion Collection.

*The Hidden Fortress* [*Kakushi-toride no san-akunin*]. Directed by Akira Kurosawa (black and white, 1958, 139 minutes). Criterion Collection.

*High and Low* [*Tengoku to jigoku*]. Directed by Akira Kurosawa (black and white, 1963, 143 minutes). Criterion Collection.

*The Idiot* [*Hakuchi*]. Directed by Akira Kurosawa (black and white, 1951, 166 minutes). Included in *Post-War Kurosawa*, Criterion Eclipse Series.

*Ikiru*. Directed by Akira Kurosawa (black and white, 1952, 143 minutes). Criterion Collection.

*Kagemusha*. Directed by Akira Kurosawa (color, 1980, 180 minutes). Criterion
   Collection.

*Kurosawa: A Documentary on the Acclaimed Director*. Directed by Adam Low
   (color, 2001, 125 minutes, plus 90 minutes of bonus interview footage).
   Wellspring Media.

*The Lower Depths* [*Donzoko*]. Directed by Akira Kurosawa (black and white,
   1957, 137 minutes). Criterion Collection.

*Madadayo*. Directed by Akira Kurosawa (color, 1993, 134 minutes). Included in
   *AK 100: 25 films of Akira Kurosawa*, Criterion Collection.

*The Men Who Tread on the Tiger's Tail* [*Tora no o wo fumu otokotachi*]. Directed
   by Akira Kurosawa (black and white, 1945, 59 minutes). Included in *The First
   Films of Akira Kurosawa*, Criterion Eclipse Series.

*A Message from Akira Kurosawa: For Beautiful Movies* (Hisao Kurosawa, 2000) is
   included as a special feature on the Criterion edition of *Ikiru*.

*The Most Beautiful* [*Ichiban utsukushiku*]. Directed by Akira Kurosawa (black
   and white, 1944, 85 minutes). Included in *The First Films of Akira Kurosawa*
   Criterion Eclipse Series.

*No Regrets for Our Youth* [*Waga seishun ni kuinashi*]. Directed by Akira
   Kurosawa (black and white, 1946, 110 minutes). Included in *Post-War
   Kurosawa* Criterion Eclipse Series.

*One Wonderful Sunday* [*Subarashiki nichiyobi*]. Directed by Akira Kurosawa
   (black and white, 1947, 109 minutes). Included in *Post-War Kurosawa*,
   Criterion Eclipse Series.

*The Quiet Duel* [*Shizukanaru ketto*]. Directed by Akira Kurosawa (black and
   white, 1949, 95 minutes). BCI Eclipse.

*Ran*. Directed by Akira Kurosawa (color, 1985, 160 minutes). Criterion Collection.

*Rashomon*. Directed by Akira Kurosawa (black and white, 1950, 88 minutes).
   Criterion Collection.

*Record of a Living Being* [*Ikimono no kiroku*]. Directed by Akira Kurosawa (black
   and white, 1955, 103 minutes) included in *Post-War Kurosawa*, Criterion
   Eclipse Series.

*Red Beard* [*Akahige*]. Directed by Akira Kurosawa (black and white, 1965,
   185 minutes). Criterion Collection.

*Rhapsody in August* [*Hachi-gatsu no kyoshikyoku*]. Directed by Akira Kurosawa
   (color, 1991, 98 minutes). MGM Home Entertainment.

*Sanjuro* [*Tsubaki Sanjuro*]. Directed by Akira Kurosawa (black and white, 1962,
   96 minutes). Criterion Collection.

*Sanshiro Sugata* [*Sugata Sanshiro*]. Directed by Akira Kurosawa (black and white,
   1943, 80 minutes). Included in *The First Films of Akira Kurosawa*, Criterion
   Eclipse Series.

*Sanshiro Sugata Part Two* [*Zoku Sugata Sanshiro*]. Directed by Akira Kurosawa (black and white, 1945, 83 minutes). Included in *The First Films of Akira Kurosawa*, Criterion Eclipse Series.

*Scandal* [*Shubun*]. Directed by Akira Kurosawa (black and white, 1950, 105 minutes). Included in *Post-War Kurosawa*, Criterion Eclipse Series.

*Seven Samurai* [*Shichinin no samurai*]. Directed by Akira Kurosawa (black and white, 1954, 207 minutes). Criterion Collection.

*Stray Dog* [*Nora inu*]. Directed by Akira Kurosawa (black and white, 1949, 122 minutes). Criterion Collection.

*Throne of Blood* [*Kumonosu-jo*]. Directed by Akira Kurosawa (black and white, 1957, 110 minutes). Criterion Collection.

*Yojimbo* [*Yojinbo*]. Directed by Akira Kurosawa (black and white, 1961, 110 minutes). Criterion Collection.


*Chapter Five: Mikio Naruse*

*Floating Clouds* [*Ukigumo*]. Directed by Mikio Naruse (black and white, 1955, 123 minutes). BFI.

*Meshi*. Directed by Mikio Naruse (black and white, 1951, 96 minutes). Eureka/ Masters of Cinema Series.

*Sound of the Mountain* [*Yama no oto*]. Directed by Mikio Naruse (black and white, 1954, 94 minutes). Eureka/Masters of Cinema Series.

*When a Woman Ascends the Stairs* [*Onna ga kaidan wo agaru toki*]. Directed by Mikio Naruse (black and white, 1960, 110 minutes). Criterion Collection.


*Chapter Six: Remembering the War*

*The Burmese Harp* [*Biruma no tategoto*]. Directed by Kon Ichikawa (black and white, 1956, 116 minutes). Criterion Collection.

*Fires on the Plain* [*Nobi*]. Directed by Kon Ichikawa (black and white, 1959, 104 minutes). Criterion Collection.

*The Human Condition* [*Ningen no joken*]. Directed by Masaki Kobayashi (widescreen black and white, 1959–61, 574 minutes). Criterion Collection.

# Bibliography

Anderson, Joseph L., and Donald Richie. *The Japanese Film: Art and Industry*, expanded ed. Princeton, NJ: Princeton University Press, 1982.

Barthes, Roland. *Empire of Signs*. Trans. Richard Howard. New York: Hill and Wang, 1982.

Bazin, André. *What Is Cinema?* Trans. Hugh Gray. Berkeley: University of California Press, 1967.

Bock, Audie. *Japanese Film Directors*. Tokyo: Kodansha, 1978.

Bordwell, David. *Ozu and the Poetics of Cinema*. Princeton, NJ: Princeton University Press, 1988.

———. *Planet Hong Kong: Popular Cinema and the Art of Entertainment*. Cambridge, MA: Harvard University Press, 2000.

Bordwell, David, Janet Staiger and Kristin Thompson. *The Classical Hollywood Cinema: Film Style and Mode of Production to 1960*. New York: Columbia University Press, 1985.

Bornoff, Nicholas. *Pink Samurai: Love, Marriage and Sex in Contemporary Japan*. New York: Pocket Books, 1991.

Brooks, Peter. *The Melodramatic Imagination: Balzac, Henry James, Melodrama, and the Mode of Excess*. New York: Columbia University Press, 1976.

Burch, Noël. *To the Distant Observer: Form and Meaning in the Japanese Cinema*. Berkeley: University of California Press, 1979.

Cavanaugh, Carole, "'Sanchô Dayû' and the Overthrow of History." In *Sanchô Dayû*, edited by Dudley Andrew and Carole Cavanaugh, 11–40. London: British Film Institute, 2000.

Cazdyn, Eric. *The Flash of Capital: Film and Geopolitics in Japan*. Durham, NC: Duke University Press, 2002.

Chung, Hye Seung. "Toward a Strategic Korean Cinephilia: A Transnational

Détournement of Hollywood Melodrama." In *South Korean Golden Age Melodrama: Gender, Genre and National Cinema*, edited by Kathleen McHugh and Nancy Abelmann, 117–50. Detroit, MI: Wayne State University Press, 2005.

Davis, Darell William. *Picturing Japaneseness: Monumental Style, National Identity, Japanese Film*. New York: Columbia University Press, 1996.

Deleuze, Gilles. *Cinema One: The Movement Image*. Trans. Hugh Tomlinson and Barbara Habberjam. Minneapolis: University of Minnesota Press, 1986.

Desser, David, ed. *Ozu's Tokyo Story*. New York: Cambridge University Press, 1997.

Dissanayake, Wimal, ed. *Melodrama and Asian Cinema*. New York: Cambridge University Press, 1993.

Douchet, Jean. "About Naruse," *Trafic* no. 3 (1992), rpt. in Hasumi and Yamane eds., *Mikio Naruse*, 98.

Ericson, Joan. *Be a Woman: Hayashi Fumiko and Modern Japanese Women's Literature*. Honolulu: University of Hawaii Press, 1997.

Fessler, Susanna. *Wandering Heart: The Work and Method of Hayashi Fumiko*. Albany: State University of New York Press, 1998.

Fujimoto, Sanezumi. "Producer Sanezumi Fujimoto," in Hasumi and Yamane eds., *Mikio Naruse*, 183.

Futaba, Juzabura. "Review of *Meshi*," *Kinema Junpo* (January 1, 1952): 116, trans. Guy Yasko.

Galbraith, Stuart, IV. *The Emperor and the Wolf: The Lives and Films of Akira Kurosawa and Toshiro Mifune*. London: Faber and Faber, 2001.

Gerow, Aaron. "The Word Before the Image: Criticism, the Screenplay and the Regulation of Meaning in Prewar Japanese Film Culture." In *Word and Image in Japanese Cinema*, edited by Dennis Washburn and Carole Cavanaugh, 3–35. Cambridge: Cambridge University Press, 2001.

———. *Visions of Japanese Modernity: Articulations of Cinema, Nation, and Spectatorship, 1895–1925*. Berkeley: University of California Press, 2010.

Gledhill, Christine. "Rethinking Genre." In *Reinventing Film Studies*, edited by Christine Gledhill and Linda Williams, 206–20. London: Arnold; New York: Oxford University Press, 2000.

Gordon, Andrew, ed. *Postwar Japan as History*. Berkeley: University of California Press, 1993.

Hansen, Miriam. "The Mass Production of the Senses: Classical Cinema as Vernacular Modernism." In *Reinventing Film Studies*, edited by Christine Gledhill and Linda Williams, 332–50. London: Arnold; New York: Oxford University Press, 2000.

——. "Fallen Women, Rising Stars, New Horizons: Shanghai Silent Film as Vernacular Modernism," *Film Quarterly* 54, no. 1 (2000): 10–22.

Harootunian, Harry. "'Detour to the East': Noël Burch and the Task of Japanese Film." Centre for Japanese Studies, University of Michigan. Available at: http://www.cjspubs.lsa.umich.edu/electronic/facultyseries/list/series/distantobserver.php (accessed August 2010).

Hasumi, Shigehiko. "Mikio Naruse or Double Signature." Hasumi, Shigehiko and Yamane Sadao, eds. *Mikio Naruse*. San Sebastian-Madrid: Festival Internacional de Cine de San Sebastian, 1998.

Hasumi, Shigehiko, and Yamane Sadao, eds. *Mikio Naruse*. San Sebastian-Madrid: Festival Internacional de Cine de San Sebastian, 1998.

Hayashi, Fumiko. *Floating Clouds*. Trans. Y. Koitabashi and M. C. Collcutt. Tokyo: Hara Publishing, 1965.

Hayashi, Sharon H. "Traveling Film History: Language and Landscape in the Japanese Cinema, 1931–45." PhD Diss., University of Chicago, 2003.

Hirano, Kyoko. *Mr. Smith Goes to Tokyo: Japanese Cinema under the American Occupation, 1945–52*. Washington, DC: Smithsonian Press, 1992.

Kawabata, Yasunari. *The Sound of the Mountain*. Trans. Edward G. Seidensticker. Tokyo: Charles E. Tuttle, 1970.

Iijima, Tadashi. "Naruse Mikio to *Onna ga kaidan o agaru toki* (Naruse Mikio and *When a Woman Ascends the Stairs*)," *Eiga Hyoron* (February 1960): 38–9, trans. Kumi Hishikawa.

Ivy, Marilyn. *Discourses of the Vanishing: Modernity, Phantasm, Japan*. Chicago: Chicago University Press, 1995.

Kirihara, Donald. *Patterns of Time: Mizoguchi and the 1930s*. Madison: Wisconsin University Press, 1992.

Kurosawa, Akira. *Something Like an Autobiography*. New York, NY: Random House, 1982.

Mellen, Joan. *Seven Samurai*, London: BFI Publishing, 2002.

Mikawa, Kiyo. "*Yama no oto*: kyokan sasou yome no tachiba (*Sound of the Mountain*: Sympathy for The Status of a Daughter-in-Law)," *Yomiuri Shinbun* (January 31, 1954): 5, trans. Chika Kinoshita.

Mizuta, Noriko. "In Search of a Lost Paradise: The Wandering Woman in Hayashi Fumiko's *Drifting Clouds*." In *The Woman's Hand: Gender and Theory in Japanese Women's Writing*, edited by Paul Gordon Schalow and Janet A. Walker, 329–51. Stanford, CA: Stanford University Press, 1996.

Mulvey, Laura. "Notes on Sirk and Melodrama" In *Home is Where the Heart Is: Studies in Melodrama and the Women's Film*, edited by Christine Gledhill, 75–9. London: British Film Institute, 1987.

Murakawa, Hide. *Naruse Mikio Enshutsujutsu: Yakusha ga kataru engi no genba*

[Naruse Mikio's Directorial Technique: Actors Talk About Acting]. Trans. Guy Yasko. Tokyo: Waizu Shuppan, 1997.

Nogami, Teruyo. *Waiting on the Weather: Making Movies with Akira Kurosawa*. Trans. Juliet Winters Carpenter. Berkeley, CA: Stone Bridge Press, 2006.

Nolletti, Arthur, Jr., and David Desser, eds. *Reframing Japanese Cinema: Authorship, Genre, History*. Bloomington: Indiana University Press, 1992.

Nygren, Scott. *Time Frames: Japanese Cinema and the Unfolding of History*. Minneapolis: University of Minnesota Press, 2007.

Oshima, Nagisa. *Cinema, Censorship, and the State: The Writings of Nagisa Oshima*. Trans. Dawn Lawson. Cambridge, MA: MIT Press, 1992.

——."The Defeated Have No Images: Had Television Existed at the End of the War," *Review of Japanese Culture and Society* 21 (December 2009): 7–17, trans Sachiko Mizuno.

Prasad, M. Madhava. *Ideology of the Hindi Film: A Historical Construction*. Oxford: Oxford University Press, 1998.

Prince, Stephen. *The Warrior's Camera: The Cinema of Akira Kurosawa*. Princeton, NJ: Princeton University Press, 1991.

Quandt, James, ed. *Kon Ichikawa*. Toronto: Cinematheque Ontario, 2001.

Ray, Robert B. *How a Film Theory Got Lost and Other Mysteries in Cultural Studies*. Bloomington: Indiana University Press, 2001.

——. "The Bordwell Regime and the Stakes of Knowledge," in *How a Film Theory Got Lost and Other Mysteries in Cultural Studies*, 29–63. Bloomington: Indiana University Press, 2001.

Richie, Donald. *Ozu*. Berkeley: University of California Press, 1974.

——. *The Films of Akira Kurosawa*. 3rd ed, Berkeley: University of California Press, 1998.

——. *A Hundred Years of Japanese Cinema*. Tokyo: Kodasha International, 2001.

Russell, Catherine. *Naruse Mikio: Women and Japanese Modernity*. Durham, NC: Duke University Press, 2009.

Sakai, Naoki. "'You Asians': On the Historical Role of the West and Asia Binary." In *Japan After Japan: Social and Cultural Life from the Recessionary 1990s to the Present*, edited by Tomioko Yoda and Harry Harootunian, 167–94. Durham, NC: Duke University Press, 2006.

Sandler, Mark, ed. *The Confusion Era: Art and Culture of Japan during the Allied Occupation, 1945–52*. Washington, DC: Smithsonian Institute, 1997.

Satō, Tadao. *Currents in Japanese Cinema*. Trans. Gregory Barrett. Tokyo: Kodansha, 1982.

Shimazu, Naoko. "Popular Representations of the Past: The Case of Postwar Japan," *Journal of Contemporary History* 38, no. 1 (January 2003): 101–16.

Shimizu, Chiyota. "Review of *Meshi (Repast)*," *Kinema Junpo* (December 1, 1951): 43, trans. Guy Yasko.

Silver, Alain. *The Samurai Film.* New York: Overlook, 1983.

Singer, Ben. *Melodrama and Modernity.* New York: Columbia University Press, 2000.

Sontag, Susan. "Fascinating Fascism." In *A Susan Sontag Reader.* New York: Farrar/Straus/Giroux, 1982: 305–25.

Springer, Julian, and Alastair Phillips, eds. *Japanese Cinema: Texts and Contexts.* London: Routledge, 2007.

Takami, Jun. "Kanso [Impressions]," *Fujin Koron* (March 1954): 222, trans. Chika Kinoshita.

Toda, Takao. Review of *Meshi (A Married Life*, a.k.a. *Repast), Eiga Hyōron* (January 1952): 85–6, trans. Guy Yasko.

Wada-Marciano, Mitsuyo. *Nippon Modern: Japanese Cinema of the 1920s and 1930s.* Honolulu: University of Hawaii Press, 2008.

———, ed. *Review of Japanese Culture and Society, Unfinished Business: The Endless Postwar in Japanese Cinema and Visual Culture* 21 (December 2009).

Williams, Christopher. "After the Classic, the Classical and Ideology: The Differences of Realism." In *Reinventing Film Studies*, edited by Christine Gledhill and Linda Williams, 206–20. London: Arnold; New York: Oxford University Press, 2000.

Williams, Linda. "Discipline and Fun." In *Reinventing Film Studies*, edited by Christine Gledhill and Linda Williams, 351–70. London: Arnold; New York: Oxford University Press, 2000.

———. *Playing the Race Card: Melodramas of Black and White from Uncle Tom to O. J. Simpson.* Princeton, NJ: Princeton University Press, 2001.

Wilson, Rob. "Spectral Critiques: Tracking 'Uncanny' Filmic Paths Towards a Bio-Poetics of Trans-Pacific Globalization." In *Hong Kong Connections: Transnational Imagination in Action Cinema*, edited by Meaghan Morris, Siu Leung Li and Stephen Chan Ching-kiu, 249–68. Durham, NC: Duke University Press, 2005.

Wilson, Sandra. "War, Soldier and Nation in 1950s Japan," *International Journal of Asian Studies* 5, no. 2 (2008): 187–218.

Yau Shuk-ting, Kinnia. "Interactions between Japanese and Hong Kong Action Cinemas." In *Hong Kong Connections: Transnational Imagination in Action Cinema*, edited by Meaghan Morris, Siu Leung Li and Stephen Chan Ching-kiu, 35–48. Durham, NC: Duke University Press, 2005.

Yoshida, Kiju. *Ozu's Anti-Cinema.* Trans. Daisuke Miyao and Kyoko Hirano. Ann Arbor: Center for Japanese Studies, University of Michigan, 2003.

Yoshimoto, Mitsuhiro. *Kurosawa: Film Studies and Japanese Cinema*. Durham, NC: Duke University Press, 2000.

——. "Logic of Sentiment: The Postwar Japanese Cinema and Questions of Modernity." PhD Diss., University of California, San Diego, 1993.

——. "Melodrama, Postmodernism and Japanese Cinema." In *Melodrama and Asian Cinema*, edited by Wimal Dissanayake, 101–26. New York: Cambridge University Press, 1993.

# Glossary

***benshi***  Japanese performers who provided live narration for silent films.

***bunraku***  A form of traditional Japanese puppet theater.

***bushido***  The samurai code of loyalty to a lord.

***chambara***  Swordplay films; the main genre of *jidai-geki*.

***deus ex machina***  A person, power or event that appears unexpectedly, saving a seemingly hopeless situation, especially as a contrived plot device in drama or fiction.

**Edo period**  The period in Japan running from 1603 to 1868.

***feminisuto***  Special brand of Japanese feminism.

***furusato***  Hometown.

***fuzokugeki***  A drama of manners.

***gendai-geki***  Contemporary drama.

***haiku***  A form of Japanese poetry.

**Heian period**  The period in Japan running from 794 to 1185.

***jidai-geki***  Period films.

***kabuki***  A form of traditional Japanese drama with song, mime and dance.

***keitai shoshetsu***  Domestic novels.

**Kempeitai**  The Japanese military police.

*kimono*   A traditional Japanese garment worn by women, men and children.

*kumi*   Group or crew.

*mama-san*   The head hostess in a bar, responsible for cultivating personal relationships with the customers.

*manga*   Graphic novels.

**Meiji period**   The period in Japan running from 1868 to 1912.

*meshi*   Often translated simply as "food," *meshi* also refers to "cooked rice" and to the simple tastes of ordinary people.

*mise en scène*   The overall design of the visual elements of a scene including the setting, the decor, the lighting, the costumes, the performance and the architecture.

*mizu shobai*   The "water trade"; traditional euphemism for the nighttime entertainment business in Japan.

*mono no aware*   The feeling of "sweet sadness" provoked by the inevitabilities of nature and mortality; the pathos of things, or the awareness of impermanence.

*naniwa-bushi*   A genre of traditional Japanese narrative singing.

*nansensu*   Nonsense.

*Noh*   A form of classical Japanese music drama with masks; traditionally all performers were male.

*obi*   A sash for traditional Japanese dress.

**OL**   Office lady.

**ronin**   A wandering samurai with no lord or master.

**sake**   A Japanese alcoholic drink made from fermented rice, traditionally served warm.

**samurai**   A member of the military nobility of feudal Japan.

*sensei*   A teacher.

*shimpa*   Meaning "new school," a form of theater usually featuring melodramatic stories.

**Shinkansen**   A high-speed railway system with passenger trains.

*shitamachi*   Meaning "low town," an area in Tokyo.

*shokai-mono*   Films with "social themes".

*shomin-geki* **or** *shoshimin-eiga*   Home drama or "films about ordinary people"; a genre derived from nineteenth-century *keitai shoshetsu* and *shimpa* drama and a key form of *gendai-geki*.

*sinp'a*   Used in South Korea to designate old-fashioned melodrama derived from the Japanese theatrical mode that was influential in the 1920s.

*tabi*   White socks that are worn with *kimono* and sandals.

*taishu engeki*   A form of theater that belongs to the working and lower middle classes, specific to modern Japan.

*tatami*   A mat used as a traditional form of Japanese floor covering.

**tendency film**   A subgenre of *gendai-geki* showing up social tendencies of inequality.

*ukigusa*   Duckweeds.

This book is due for return on or before the last date shown below.